Secrets of the Frontline Superstars

Marlene Caroselli, Ed.D.

SkillPath Publications
Mission, Kansas

Project Editor: Bill Cowles

Cover and Book Design: Jason Sprenger
                        Willa Sleyster

ISBN: 1-929874-42-1

10   9   8   7   6   5   4   3   2   06   07

Printed in the United States of America

CONTENTS

INTRODUCTION

Imagination takes vision out of its tunnel! And once freed from a confining space, vision can become an innovative reality. Imagination is not the private domain of the rare few who are able to see something new while others look at something old. Creative skills can be honed by anyone—despite the assertion of those self-doubting individuals who proclaim there's not a single creative bone in their bodies.

In times of restructuring, reengineering, and reinventing, administrative professionals are discovering their own "re-" word: "redefining." The redefinition began with giving Professional Secretaries International (PSI), a new title: The International Association of Administrative Professionals (IAAP). Look for an interview with IAAP's former president, Amelia Barclay, later in the book.

While many administrative professionals (or "admins" as they are often called) still prefer and go by the term "secretary" or "support staff," most feel the "administrative professional" title is a better reflection of both the nature and the contributions of their work. For purposes of inclusiveness, brevity, and readability throughout the book, we'll use the term admins.

Secrets of the Frontline Superstars is the successor to our earlier book, *The Innovative Secretary*, and reflects the changes that are happening in the world of administrative professionals. Because we seem to live in an age of paradox, we face both constant changes and constant constants—that is, there are some things that will *not* change. In our earlier research, we identified 25 traits associated with innovative thinking that are constant constants. Because they are constant, we have retained these traits and the skill building exercises associated with them. The interviews at the end of each section offer contemporary real-life examples of how the traits apply to successful administrative professionals, many of whom are familiar names in the business world. Together, the traits, interviews and exercises embody the secrets of success for all frontline superstars—including you!

The interviews asked outstanding representatives of the administrative professional field to share their thoughts on seven important questions.

1. Given these traits, which do you feel is most important for administrative professionals and why?

Tolerates confusion	Is persistent
Is willing to explore	Is self-confident
Is receptive to new ideas	Is patient with ideas
Sees the invisible	Is resourceful
Sees problems as opportunities	Is entrepreneurial
Is self-directed	Dislikes routine
Defers judgment	Can juggle tasks
Concentrates well	Thinks fluidly
Thinks divergently	Has original thoughts
Has a child's mind	Uses metaphors
Escapes mental restraints	Probes ideas deeply
Sees the big picture	Bravely non-conforms
Copes with rejection	

2. How do you handle the stress associated with your job?

3. It's been said that results depend on relationships. What suggestions do you have for optimizing one's relationship with one's manager and other key players at work?

4. What macrocosmic challenges facing the nation may be microcosmically affecting the way today's administrative professional work?

5. The only constant, it seems, is change. In some organizations, in fact, the descriptive sentence is "No sooner said ... than changed!" What can administrative professionals do to accept—perhaps even embrace—change?

6. What "lessons learned" can you share with others on how to be a "frontline superstar"?

7. The following quotation by Warren Bennis underscores the importance of being a continuous learner:

   "The factory of the future will have only two employees, a man and a dog. The man will be there to feed the dog. The dog will be there to keep the man from touching the equipment."

What advice can you give regarding updating one's skills?

Responding to these questions are:

- *Colleen Barrett*, President and Chief Operating Officer of Southwest Airlines and a former legal secretary.

- *Nancy Parent*, Office Manager for the Department of Research, Evaluation and Testing, City School District, Rochester, New York.

- *Amelia Barclay*, former International President of the International Association of Administrative Professionals (IAAP).

- *Roberta L. Carter*, CPS (Certified Professional Secretary), who supports the Vice President of Human Resources in the Production Systems Group, Xerox Corporation, Rochester, New York. (You'll learn what she means by "supports" when you read the stress-question reply in her interview.)

We also include a composite interview from a team working at the Human Resource Service Center, Southwest, Department of the Navy, San Diego, California. They are:

- *Eleanor Bautista*, Human Resources Assistant

- *Charlotte Easter*, Human Resources Assistant

- *Angela Robinson*, Human Resources Assistant

- *Jennifer Martinez*, Human Resources Specialist

- *Yvonne Young-Dong*, Human Resources Specialist

We wish you well on your journey to frontline excellence. And, we encourage you to use your leadership talents to discuss these traits with peers and supervisors. Further, we hope you'll do the exercises whenever you and other administrative professionals assemble. There's strength in numbers and you can begin to number your strength as you gain practice and self-confidence. That superstar shining within the firmament of your organization belongs to you. Hitch your career wagon to it.

TOLERATES CONFUSION

C reative people tolerate ambiguity well, knowing that in time the ambiguous state will become better defined. They are comfortable when presented with the unknown. In fact, they often feel exhilarated as they contemplate a new problem. Complexity, opposing thoughts, vague outcomes—these do not daunt the creative individual who feels a heady excitement at the prospect of pushing existing boundaries.

Just as our ancestors became explorers and immigrants, creative people have the pioneering spirit that encourages moving beyond the known to the unknown, tearing down existing barriers in order to see new vistas.

One technique you can practice to bring you closer to an idealized state is to engage in fantasy. Fantasizing helps you to let go of the need for exactitude and to feel comfortable in situations that may not be well-defined. Don't underestimate the power of the imagination. Should you start to feel guilty for daydreaming, remember Einstein's words: "When I examined myself and my methods of thought, I came to the conclusion that the gift of fantasy has meant more to me than my talent for absorbing knowledge."

EXERCISE:

Tolerate ambiguity by fantasizing.

If you wish to increase your capacity for imagining, try engaging in fantasy from time to time. What would you imagine as an administrative professional's dream scenario? Record your thoughts after reading the samples provided.

> *"Good morning, Mr. X! Let me remind you that your first conference today will start within ten minutes. You'll meet our technical division people on the second floor. All the material you need for this presentation is on your table. After the conference, I'll give you the messages from last week. Would you like anything else before you leave?"*

What are your impressions of the admin in this fantasy? Within six sentences, a distinct image has been created. Do you see a partnership at work, born of respect for and consideration of everyone's needs and talents? You may also have noticed a crisp efficiency operating as well.

The following fantasy, however, projects a different impression.

> *"Good morning, Ms. X! You're a few minutes late for our meeting but don't worry. I know how terrible traffic can be. Before we begin, would you mind getting me a cup of coffee. With cream … that's right. [Pause.] Thank you. Oh, you'll need your steno pad—I have quite a few points to make. To begin, we have to institute a 20 percent raise for me—effective immediately. Next, I have been thinking about your proposal to hire an assistant for me. I've come to the conclusion that you are correct—I am overworked. So, yes, let's proceed with that. Finally, I'd like to have some business cards made. Could you handle that for me? The title? 'Administrative Executive' will be fine!"*

6

What would your perfect scenario be like? Be creative. You can't achieve something you cannot imagine. Record your thoughts here:

"Good morning, Ms. X!

_____

_____

_____

_____

_____

_____

_____

_____

_____

_____

_____ "

EXERCISE:

Tolerate ambiguity by bridging existing and future states.

It's been said that nothing is as real as a dream. In the preceeding exercise, you fantasized a future state with conditions quite different from those you work in today. One way to bring your dreams closer to your realities is to bridge existing and future states. In other words, what would it take to have tomorrow's dream supplant today's reality?

Yes, the future is uncertain. Ambiguity surrounds the present. It is true that no one really knows what's in store for our world, our country, our organization, ourselves. And yet, we all have the capacity to influence the future, to shape the circumstances that could easily become reality. That's what vision is all about.

There was a time, for instance, when there were no professional organizations for secretaries. There was a time when the Certified Professional Secretaries (CPS) degree did not exist. There was a time when the United States did not honor administrative professionals in April. But all these became realities because someone had a dream. Imaginative people can tolerate ambiguity. They have faith in their ability to carve distinct shapes from the amorphous mass known as "tomorrow."

A. List here your current job conditions. (If you prefer, you could list realities that exist for admins in general.)

   _____

   _____

   _____

B. Now explain what the ideal job would be like. (Or, in more global terms, explain what could be considered the ideal state for all admins.)

_____

_____

_____

_____

_____

_____

C. Finally, describe what it would take to create that future state. What plans must you implement? What "bridges" would you have to build in order to move from the reality of the present to the "ideality" of the future?

_____

_____

_____

_____

_____

_____

IS WILLING TO EXPLORE

The innovative admin is willing to explore new ideas, to examine new possibilities, to allow the "known" to forge a path for the "unknown." Of course, it's more secure to remain with the existing circumstances, but if our ancestors had not been willing to explore, most of us would not be here today. While it can be uncomfortable to leave the familiar behind, it can also be a rousing experience. A sense of adventure permeates the lives of those who view uncharted territory with eagerness.

EXERCISE:

Explore possibilities with a new word.

The word *secretary* has undergone significant change since the profession was born in ancient Rome. There, the secretary (derived from the word "secretarius") was a person who could be trusted with secrets. Today, of course, the secretary is still the trusted confidante, but the job includes responsibilities that go far beyond the original sphere of influence.

For years, secretaries questioned the appropriateness of the term that described their function. Alternatives, of course, had been suggested: "administrative assistant," "office administrator," "support staff specialist," and now we use "administrative professional".

For this exercise, try to come up with a brand-new word or phrase—one that no one has ever used before. One that's not in the dictionary. One that captures the true essence of what secretaries do. Just as the word "avionics" was created to depict the impact of electronics on aviation, and just as Coach Pat Riley created the word "threepeat" to describe the success of a team that wins three basketball championships in a row, so can you create a word that no one else has heard—yet.

Here are some neologisms (newly created words) to get you started:

multitary   to reflect having more than one boss

cybertary   to reflect increased computer responsibilities

paramanager   to reflect tasks increasingly managerial in nature

datalyst   to reflect work that needs a head and not just hands

What neologisms can you devise? _____

_____

_____

_____

_____

_____

_____

_____

_____

EXERCISE:

Use "what if" thinking to explore new avenues of thought.

When you engage in "what if" thinking, you force your mind to travel new pathways. This process is the stuff of which innovation is born. Consider this hypothetical situation: "What if God had had an admin?"

Some possible consequences of that subjunctive state are these:

The world would have been created in five days!

Admins would be regarded as earth angels.

Della Street and not Saint Peter would be guarding the gates of Heaven.

The word *secretary* would carry as much significance as the term *Secretary of State*.

No one would precede "admin" with the words "just an."

Now respond to the following "what if" scenario: *What if admins were paid what they are worth?*

1. "Organizations would go broke" was probably your first thought. Continue thinking … along more serious lines, if you can. Record your thoughts here:

   _____

   _____

   _____

   _____

   _____

   _____

   _____

2. Now specify one thing that you could do to make the possibility you suggested above a reality:

   _____

   _____

   _____

   _____

   _____

   _____

   _____

IS RECEPTIVE TO NEW IDEAS

maginative individuals keep their minds open—and, as a result, all kinds of ideas can fly in. In fact, it is staying receptive to new possibilities that helps them come up with new ideas. Experts tell us we should spend about one-third of our reading time perusing fields other than those we naturally gravitate to.

Innovative administrative professionals know that just because they've never heard of a person or a concept doesn't mean it doesn't exist or that it lacks value. And because they accept novelty, because they are willing to consider rather than to condemn, they not only welcome new ideas, they often create them!

EXERCISE:

Engage in "Janusian" thinking.

Janus was the ancient Roman god of the new year (hence, "January"). On coins, his face was shown looking in two directions: back over the recently passed year and forward to the new year. When you allow yourself to think in Janusian terms, you are able to look at any idea from two opposing points of view.

W. E. McMullan notes that "creative individuals are paradoxical personages." And Carl Jung has observed that "every creative person is a duality or a synthesis of contradictory aptitudes."

This exercise may bring new insights to both you and your manager. Begin by listing the things for which the typical boss is responsible for in a given week; in the next column, list the things the typical admin is responsible for in a given week:

Boss	Admin
_____	_____
_____	_____
_____	_____
_____	_____
_____	_____
_____	_____
_____	_____
_____	_____

Secrets of the Frontline Superstars

Now go back and write an "A" beside those managerial functions you feel you could handle, in part or in full. Then place an "M" beside administrative functions that a boss can, does, or should handle. (For example, typing, proofreading, and editing have long been functions of the assistant. Many a manager, however, now performs those functions—thanks to the ubiquity of the computer.)

How could you persuade your boss to let you handle more managerial tasks?

_____

_____

_____

_____

_____

_____

_____

EXERCISE:

Be receptive to kinesthetic thoughts.

You can foster creativity when you consider a particular essence not in its usual sensory terms but rather in unusual sensory terms. This crossing of sensory inputs is known as "kinesthesia." For example, many people typically think of problems as situations that can be improved with thoughtful actions. But what if you consider problems as things you can see or touch or hear? For example, what if problems were water? Here are some kinesthetic responses to that very question from support staff personnel at Johnson Controls.

"If problems were water, I'd probably be swimming every day, but at the end, I'd make sure to grab a big towel and dry off." *Jenni Mastrogiovanni*

"If problems were water, I'd be drowning because I'm in way over my head. (The plus side is that—with a pack of Kool-Aid and some sugar—I'd never be thirsty.)" *CaSandra Mathis*

"If problems were water, I would float to the top." *Luonne Dumak*

"If problems were water, there would be a rain storm in my office daily." *Kathy Halbrooks*

"If problems were water, my cup runneth over." *Murphy Nieskes*

"If problems were water, I'd use them to feed my plants." *Brigid McGeehan*

"If problems were water, a sponge could absorb them all." *Dawn Tietyen*

Now it's your turn. Just relax and allow your mind to travel along some new paths. Think about this kinesthetic possibility:

If you could see stress, it would look like _____

_____

or _____

_____

or _____

_____

or _____

_____

or _____

_____

or _____

_____

or _____

_____

Now try a kinesthetic possibility of your own:

_____

_____

_____

SEES THE INVISIBLE

A popular creativity spur is to look at what everyone else is looking at but to see what no one else is seeing. This, perhaps, is the very essence of creativity: doing the uncommon with the common, turning the familiar into the unfamiliar. We are surrounded with "reusabilities"—items that can either contribute to America's growing garbage problem or that can be put to new use. Admins who can salvage the throwaways and use them to save time, money, and the environment are the secretaries whose thinking skills are valued. Likewise, secretaries who practice looking at things and situations in uncommon ways will hone their ability to think creatively and suggest new ideas—from ways to save time on projects to streamlining office procedures.

EXERCISE:

Create new uses for old things.

Assume it's the day after Administrative Professionals Day and every admin in your organization has a vase of wilting flowers. You hate to see them headed for the wastebasket, so you decide to spearhead a drive to rescue all those flowers and do something practical with them.

Record here what you can do beyond the obvious first two. Return to the page often if you don't finish it today. Ask for suggestions from other people and then ... try implementing the best ideas next April!

1. Press them and make greeting cards with them.

2. Dry them for potpourri.

3. _____

4. _____

5. _____

6. _____

7. _____

8. _____

9. _____

10. _____

11. _____

12. _____

13. _____

14. _____

15. _____

16. _____

17. _____

18. _____

19. _____

20. _____

21. _____

22. _____

23. _____

24. _____

25. _____

EXERCISE:

Develop turnaround thinking.

"Turnaround thinking" will lead you to novel ideas—those untouched by triteness. All you need to do is take a familiar phrase or ordinary saying and turn it around so it becomes a wondrously new concept—untainted by hackneyed thought. A good example is Reverend Jesse Jackson's proclamation: "I was born in the slums but the slums were not born in me!" Or President Jimmy Carter's definition of America's genesis: "America did not invent human rights. Human rights invented America."

Here is a less serious turnaround: "Time heals all wounds" and its barbed counterpart, "Time wounds all heels." And an even less serious one: "I used to be lost in the shuffle. Now I just shuffle with the lost." Finally, delight in this from a frustrated but unknown member of Congress: "You can bring a House to order, but you can't make it think."

Think about the administrative function and give it a fresh twist by turning around one (or more) of these common phrases:

add insult to injury	benefit of the doubt
all in a day's work	better late than never
all things being equal	bite off more than you can chew
as luck would have it	bite the bullet
ax to grind	bring home the bacon
bark up the wrong tree	can't see the forest for the trees
beat around the bush	cool as a cucumber
bend over backward	diamond in the rough
down in the dumps	handwriting on the wall

easier said than done	hard row to hoe
face the music	hit the nail on the head
fate worse than death	hook, line, and sinker
feather in your cap	in the final analysis
feeling your oats	in the nick of time
flash in the pan	irons in the fire
get a foot in the door	knock on wood

_____

_____

_____

_____

_____

_____

_____

_____

_____

_____

_____

SEES PROBLEMS AS OPPORTUNITIES

The founder of L. L. Bean loved to hunt, but he hated coming home with wet leather boots. He used his discomfort to lead him to a solution—putting leather tops on rubber bottoms. Discomfort, albeit emotional rather than physical, was also the genesis of another innovative endeavor. Edwin Land had taken his family to Santa Fe for vacation. His five-year-old daughter asked him to take her photograph, which he did, happily. She *then* asked, "Daddy, can I see it?" It was difficult for Land to deny his daughter, but her question prompted him to think: "Perhaps I could invent a camera that would develop the film itself and produce a complete photograph within minutes." Thus, the Polaroid Land Camera was born.

Success is often a function of receptivity. The average person accepts today's reality as tomorrow's reality too. The innovator, by contrast, seeks to alter today's reality, to fulfill its promise for the future. Don't permit negatives to destroy possibilities. *Regard problems as opportunities.*

From time to time, think about Paul Schoemaker, an associate professor at the University of Chicago. He contends that all decisions are influenced by the way they're phrased when they're presented. As an experiment, he presented a plan to his students and asked for their input. He told half the students that the plan had an 80 percent chance of succeeding. The other half were told the plan had a 20 percent chance of failing. This, of course, is the same statistic—just presented from two different perspectives. However, the students who heard the word *success*, by a large majority, voted to proceed with the plan. The majority of those who heard the word *failure* voted to have him abandon the plan.

"Attitude," as they say, "is all."

EXERCISE:

Develop faith that opportunities exist in problems.

The energy for creativity is born in problems—problems that push us to change the status quo and move toward a better way. If necessity is the mother of invention, challenge is the father of creativity. Each day we face an onslaught of difficulties; occasionally they overwhelm us and we fall on our faces. But we have the capacity to rise again and again to tackle the obstacles that stand in our way. That is what life is all about.

The most resilient among us have found ways to meet challenges and sometimes even to profit from them. This exercise is designed to deepen your awareness of the silver linings that await just inside most "clouds."

Think about your life over the last five or ten years and list the most serious problems you can recall from that time span:

1. _____

_____

2. _____

_____

3. _____

_____

4. _____

_____

5. _____

_____

6. _____

_____

7. _____

_____

8. _____

_____

9. _____

_____

10. _____

_____

11. _____

_____

12. _____

_____

13. _____

_____

14. _____

_____

15. _____

_____

Now go back and write an "O" beside each problem that had some positive result—some way in which you grew or were able to help others or became a stronger person or learned something beneficial. How many of those original problems were actually opportunities in disguise?

EXERCISE:

Look at problems from a new perspective.

One problem-solving technique that sometimes leads to innovative results is the "3F approach": Flaws, Failures, and Faults. Begin by briefly describing a problem you're currently facing: _____

_____

_____

_____

Quickly list some solutions for this problem: _____

_____

_____

_____

Now choose the best of the above solutions and think of it in terms of the "3Fs."

Flaws

Imagine that your most severe critic were to find flaws in this solution. What flaws would that person cite? _____

_____

_____

_____

_____

As you review the flaws you expect a critic to point out, isolate one that might be legitimate. Use it to stimulate some action you might have forgotten to take, and specify that action here: _____

_____

_____

_____

Failure

How could this solution backfire? What might go wrong? What would happen if you tried to implement this solution and you failed miserably? List all the negative consequences you can think of:

_____

_____

_____

If your decision/solution does fail, what is one positive result that you would realize? _____

_____

Faults

If the solution you are proposing were implemented and if the effects were damaging—disastrous even—who or what would be considered "at fault"?

_____

_____

How could that blame be minimized or lessened? What precautions could be taken to soften the blow of accusations, even if the solution did not work as planned? _____

_____

_____

Assume all fingers were pointing at you as the person responsible for this poor decision. What benefits could you derive from an experience such as this? _____

_____

With the 3F method, you can learn to minimize mistakes by looking at your pending decision as a *fait accompli*. Even with careful, creative forethought, though, mistakes will occur. Whether or not you can then put a "positive spin" on these mistakes will depend on your attitude. Let these words of wisdom help you form that attitude:

"Stumbling is not falling."

Portuguese proverb

"He who has never made a mistake is one who never does anything."

Theodore Roosevelt

"If I wasn't making mistakes, I wasn't making decisions."

Robert W. Johnson

INTERVIEW:

Colleen Barrett, President and Chief Operating Officer of Southwest Airlines, Dallas, Texas

Q: *Given these traits, which do you feel is most important for administrative professionals and why?*

A: All the suggestions are good traits for a successful administrative professional, but two stand out in my mind. First, be willing to explore. Don't just do the job you've been assigned, but consider what else might need to be done to help make the person you are supporting more successful. Don't feel confined by boundaries; explore your surroundings and the environment and determine what else you could be doing to add value to the organization and the person you are charged with "keeping straight."

Second, bravely non-conform. Being an administrative assistant doesn't mean that there has to be a pre-conceived notion of the value you bring to the position. Anticipate a need, provide a solution for a challenge, and make suggestions for increased productivity. Bravely break down the stereotypical definitions that might exist and discover what you can do to make a positive difference.

Q: *How do you handle the stress associated with your job?*

A: My few "escapes" include reading romance novels, taking regular swims in my backyard pool, playing with my two dogs, or spending a quiet evening of conversation with close friends and family members.

Secrets of the Frontline Superstars

Q: It's been said that results depend on relationships. What suggestions to you have for optimizing one's relationship with one's manager and other key players at work?

A: Relationships are key in any successful partnership, including those of boss/employee or administrative professional/boss. I have been most fortunate to have a boss in Herb Kelleher (attorney who co-founded Southwest Airlines and is its current executive chairman). He is a wonderful mentor and friend. It was second nature to him to involve me in the cases on which he was working.

I never knew that it was unusual for a legal secretary to accompany an attorney to the courtroom, but Herb was open to my involvement. That opened my eyes to the importance of relationships. At Southwest Airlines (SWA) we have a unique corporate culture that is built on relationships and The Golden Rule. All levels of management have a teamwork ethic and "can do" attitude that we believe helps us motivate and provide resources for the frontline employees. They are the ones who are out there providing millions of people outstanding customer service and making it possible for them to be with friends and loved ones for the truly important events in their lives.

Q: What macrocosmic challenges facing the nation may be microcosmically affecting the way you work?

A: The events of September 11 had a profound effect on the airline industry. The creation of the U.S. Department of Homeland Security was the catalyst for many changes in the way airlines operate, and that has certainly lead to many changes at Southwest and the way we do business. I marvel at how resilient our employees have been to changing security directives, new technology, new processes and procedures, and a new national airport security workforce of the Transportation Security Administration.

Certainly the myriad of changes in technology and homeland security has impacted how I work. We must be flexible to the changing rules; we must be prepared to respond quickly to changes in national threat levels; and we must take time to educate our customers on those changes, as well as all the new technology we have introduced (such as our Rapid Check-In kiosks, computer-generated boarding cards, and our new gate readers).

Q: *The only constant, it seems, is change. In some organizations, in fact, the descriptive sentence is "No sooner said ... than changed!" What can administrative professionals do to accept—perhaps even embrace—change?*

A: I have the advantage of many years in the airline industry, so change is constant and never a shock to me! Our flexibility and nimbleness as a Company allow us the ability to change directions quickly and capitalize on competitive opportunities as they come along. Again, our corporate culture embraces individuals and teams that thrive on the excitement of the ever-changing airline industry. Every employee is empowered to find a creative solution to a challenge. That empowerment makes us open to change that leads to things working more productively and efficiently.

Q: *What "lessons learned" can you share with others on how to be a "frontline superstar"?*

A: I had the good fortune while a legal secretary to be involved in what was going on. I never knew it was unusual to do the many things I did as a legal secretary (like accompany an attorney to court), so I just took every opportunity I could to learn. It's a willingness to learn and a commitment to be a lifelong learner that will make you a "superstar" with whomever you're working and in any capacity.

Q: *What advice can you give regarding updating one's skills?*

A: Of course it's important to keep up with technology and embrace processes that make our jobs more efficient and productive. But, in doing so, it is critically important to not be high-tech at the expense of high-touch. I always caution our people that we cannot let technology replace the high level of personal customer service for which we have become famous.

While there might be technological solutions that make the delivery of customer service more expedient, we have to remember that no technology is necessary to offer a smile, a helping hand, and a sense of warmth and caring. It's that level of service that sets Southwest apart from its competitors, and no amount of technology or "skills updating" will make that delivery any easier or more genuine.

Of course, each executive is going to have his/her own list of preferred skills that make an employee a perfect fit for a given organization, but here is a short list of the "ideals" I would look for in the perfect administrative assistant:

- Golden-Rule behavior
- Desire to make a positive difference
- Self-starter attitude
- Anticipation of needs
- Solutions-orientation
- Resourcefulness and self-motivation
- Big-picture thinker (but-detail oriented as well)
- Passion and vision about the "SWA cause"
- Team player
- Altruism
- Whatever-it-takes outlook

Is
SELF-DIRECTED

Innovative employees are inner-directed; they are entrepreneurial in spirit. They'd prefer to be given a general direction rather than detailed directions. Innovative admins like having trust placed in them, for trust means faith in their judgment and in their capability. There are attendant risks, of course: When someone else makes all the decisions, that person derives both the glory of success and the responsibility for failure. When you make the decisions, you derive the glory and the responsibility.

Human beings, like ships, are safe if they never leave the harbor. But also like ships, people weren't created to stay in harbors.

EXERCISE:

Test your S-D (self-direction) quotient.

A. Place an "X" in the column that indicates how each statement applies to you.

	Not at all	Somewhat	Absolutely
1. I like saying, "I did it my way."	☐	☐	☐
2. I'm known as a self-starter.	☐	☐	☐
3. I prefer direction to directions.	☐	☐	☐
4. I am a careful risk-taker.	☐	☐	☐
5. Achievement is important to me.	☐	☐	☐
6. I like having responsibility.	☐	☐	☐
7. I often take the initiative to get things started.	☐	☐	☐
8. I like being in charge.	☐	☐	☐
9. I cherish personal freedom.	☐	☐	☐
10. I am highly motivated.	☐	☐	☐
11. I am flexible and open-minded.	☐	☐	☐
12. I welcome feedback on my performance.	☐	☐	☐
13. I often assume the leadership role.	☐	☐	☐
14. I have a high energy level.	☐	☐	☐

B. Which of these scenarios comes closest to your interpretation of this picture?

1. This woman has finished organizing the retirement party for a co-worker. All the committees she set up have done what they had to do (except the cleanup committee). The final and most pleasant task was to purchase a gift with the moneys she collected. In a few hours, the fun will begin.

2. This woman understands the importance of occasional self-indulgence. She'd promised herself that once she'd completed a long and tedious project, she would reward herself. She completed the project on time and under budget, and she's rewarded herself for this outstanding accomplishment.

3. This woman likes nothing better than socializing. She's always being invited to get-togethers and, it seems, is always having them herself. On this occasion, with her "hostess gift" in hand, she's on her way to a friend's house for a holiday gathering.

Interpreting your responses:
In section A, how many "not at all" answers did you have? _____

If you had seven or more, you're probably more comfortable being directed by others than directing yourself. Certainly, there's nothing wrong with this preference. However, it will be difficult to become a creative achiever if you are unwilling to initiate things. If you had seven or more and if you really would like to become a creative achiever, tackle small undertakings, get feedback, and move on to more challenging tasks.

How many "somewhat" answers did you have? If you had seven or more, you have a solid foundation for innovation. People need to overcome psychological barriers before they can give their imaginations free reign. Seven or more "somewhats" indicate a willingness on your part to accept challenges. Many of those challenges will be ones you have established for yourself.

How many "absolutely" answers did you have? If you had seven or more, you are allowing your imagination to lead the way to new ventures and adventures. Channel that intellectual energy and focus it on situations in your office environment that need improvement.

For section B, answers 1 and 2 both indicate considerable self-direction.

Answer 3 indicates a strong interest in "affiliation" or being with other people. These assessments are based on work done over the past forty years by Harvard professor David McClelland, who uses pictures (Thematic Apperception Tests or TAT's) as a prompt to story telling. On the basis of the interpretations people make of the pictures they see, he has determined that people are driven by the need for achievement, the need to take charge, and/or the need to work with other people. There is no "right" or "wrong" need, but it's important to align these motivational needs or drives to the work you have elected to do.

EXERCISE:

Imagine directing yourself— and then work to create the reality.

"Intrapreneur" is a term Gifford Pinchot coined to describe the person who works as an entrepreneur inside an organization instead of taking his or her talents outside the organization to establish a business. When organizations make accommodations for intrapreneuring, everyone wins. The employee is given a degree of autonomy, of empowerment. For some people, this is a sine qua non as far as work is concerned. The organization profits too by retaining this talent and maximizing its potential.

But such situations do not merely happen. They begin as an idea that is carefully nurtured to fruition. Conceptualize being in charge of the office by imagining a single day during which you must direct the flow of work. Assume your boss was sent on an overseas assignment and you are left in charge of the office. Now imagine a typical day without him or her, and think about how the hours would be spent. Use the next page to list and describe those activities.

If I Were the Boss…

8:00 _____

8:30 _____

9:00 _____

9:30 _____

10:00 _____

10:30 _____

11:00 _____

11:30 _____

12:00 _____

12:30 _____

1:00 _____

1:30 _____

2:00 _____

2:30 _____

3:00 _____

3:30 _____

4:00 _____

4:30 _____

5:00 _____

Next, make a list of the phone calls you would likely receive in a typical day:

1. _____ Concerning _____

2. _____ Concerning _____

3. _____ Concerning _____

4. _____ Concerning _____

5. _____ Concerning _____

6. _____ Concerning _____

7. _____ Concerning _____

8. _____ Concerning _____

9. _____ Concerning _____

10. _____ Concerning _____

Look over the list now and place an "M" in front of the calls you could handle yourself. (Research shows that competent admins can handle 90 percent of the calls coming in to their offices.)

Think next about the written information that comes into your office each day—letters, memos, e-mail, faxes, reports, and so on. Jot down the typical day's worth of data:

1. _____

2. _____

3. _____

4. _____

5. _____

6. _____

7. _____

8. _____

9. _____

10. _____

Remembering that overseas communications can be expensive, which of the above would you need to send to your boss (place a "B" in front of the item number) and which could you handle yourself (place an "M" in front of those numbers)?

Finally, think about what it would take to convince your boss that you're capable of handling more responsibilities and fewer directions.

DEFERS JUDGMENT

T he business world abounds with verbal murderers—those who can kill a good idea by uttering a few disparaging words. Some of those ideas are so brutally destroyed there is no hope of ever resuscitating them. Don't engage in "ideacide" yourself. Before you reject a thought as too expensive, too risky, or too complicated, engage in positive scrutiny. Allow the idea to incubate. In its altered, refined form, it may be totally workable. But if you inhibit ideas in their infancy, you'll never know their potential, and you'll have no way of gauging how serious the loss is. As W. Edwards Deming has noted, "The greatest losses are unknown and unknowable."

In some teams, members are free to "shoot down" the ideas of others. But before they utter their rejecting statements, they must offer three affirming statements. They must give three advantages of the idea, three ways in which it *could work.* Try this technique at your next team meeting, whenever the team is ready to discard a possibly beneficial proposal: acknowledge three strong points the idea has, re-think it, and *then* reject it if necessary. In addition to encouraging people to offer suggestions, the ideas themselves can be explored thoroughly instead of being rejected after only a superficial examination.

EXERCISE:

Engage in "gray" thinking.

"For every complex problem," H.L. Mencken commented, "there is one solution that is simple, neat, and wrong." All too often, we seek black-and-white answers when we should be looking for answers with multiple shades of gray. As individuals, as teams, as organizations, we succumb to the pressures of time and jump to quick solutions when in-depth analysis may be called for instead.

To help you go beyond the obvious, take a look at these two words: "red" and "brown".

What do they have in common? _____

_____

You probably noted that both were colors. Did you also note that:

- Both begin with a consonant?

- Both end with a consonant?

- Both have a single vowel in the middle?

- Both have another word inside ("Ed" and "own")?

- Both contain the letter "r"?

Get some practice in going beyond the obvious black-and-white answers by writing down the commonalties these words share.

Secrets of the Frontline Superstars

1. Cadillac, Chevrolet, Camaro _____

_____

_____

_____

2. lemon, apple, lime _____

_____

_____

3. Lincoln, Jefferson, Washington _____

_____

_____

4. gazelle, rabbit, squirrel _____

_____

_____

5. nightmare, daydream, woolgathering _____

_____

_____

EXERCISE:

Ignore the "mostbusters."

There are those who—deliberately or inadvertently—will dismiss or deny the potential you have for effecting positive change. These people are "mostbusters" for they "bust" your desire to "be the most you can be." The reasons why such individuals attempt to stifle innovation are numerous, but many can be related to Max DePree's wise observation: "The creative process in today's corporation is by its very nature difficult to handle. Anything truly creative results in change, and if there is one thing a well-run bureaucracy or institution or major corporation finds difficult to handle, it is change."

When you experience rejection, when others try to "bust" your innovative efforts, remember that what you're experiencing has been experienced by countless others who had good ideas. ("Every great oak," it has been observed, "was once a nut that stood its ground.") For this perseverance-promoting exercise, match the individuals on the left with the comments others have made about them.

1. Louis Pasteur

   A. Had first manuscript rejected by sixteen literary agents and twenty-four publishing houses

2. Guiseppe Verdi

   B. Was expelled from school after the principal said, "Your mere presence offends me"

3. Walt Disney

   C. Was declared "insufficiently talented"

4. Wilma Glodean Rudolph

   D. Was deemed a "mediocre" student

5. Winston Churchill

   E. Was called a "hopeless" alcoholic

6. Grandma Moses

   F. Was regarded as "insane" for trying to turn rubber into practical use

7. Thomas Edison

   G. Was considered too old to succeed

8. Albert Einstein

   H. Was labeled "too stupid to learn"

9. Charles Goodyear

   I. Was told he had no talent

10. Bill Wilson

    J. Was termed "dull" and failed sixth grade

11. John Grisham

    K. Was told she would never be able to walk normally

1-D; 2-C; 3-I; 4-K; 5-J; 6-G; 7-H; 8-B; 9-F; 10-E; 11-A

CONCENTRATES WELL

We live in chaotic times and often work in hectic environments. Each day, each hour, each minute, we are bombarded with a great variety of stimuli. In fact, scientists tell us we can process eight hundred ideas, words, images, impressions *a minute!* All of this makes staying focused a real challenge. A great many forces intrude on concentration, and a great many sensory inputs demand our attention—which is limited at best.

The good news, though, is that you can develop strong concentration skills. With the goal clearly defined and your mental faculties attuned to that goal, you can remain centered as you attempt to accomplish whatever the job requires.

EXERCISE:

Practice concentration.

One technique that will sharpen your ability to think only about one thing at a time is a practice exercise that resembles dialing a phone. For this exercise, you will need a page of telephone numbers as well as a timer.

Assume the numbers below are the buttons of a telephone. Set your timer for two minutes.

Place a mark at the top of one column from a page of phone-book numbers and begin to dial the numbers listed. When the timer goes off, place a mark next to the last number you dialed. Practice this skill-builder whenever you have two spare minutes. See how much beyond your first effort you can go. Date each effort so you can track your progress.

EXERCISE:

Set self-challenges.

Thomas Edison set self-challenges and then worked to fulfill his own prophecies. He decided upon the number of inventions he wanted to present to the Patent Office each week. In other words, he wooed his creative abilities instead of wailing that he had none. Here is a practice exercise that will not only increase your capacity for concentration, it should also inspire you to do better with each subsequent practice.

You will need a timer for this activity, which is done in this way. Look at these letters:

[dc]   [oa]   [gt]

If you look only at the letters on the left side of each bracketed item, they will spell the word "dog." And if you look only at the letters on the right side of each bracketed item, they will spell the word "cat." Set your timer now and see how long it takes you to determine the two words (one with letters on the left side of the bracketed pair and the other with letters on the right side of each bracketed pair) contained in each line. Record your starting time here: _____

1. [m c] [o o] [d m] [e e] [r d] [a i] [t a] [e n] _____

2. [m m] [a o] [t v] [e e] [r m] [i e] [a n] [l t] _____

3. [e a] [x r] [e r] [r o] [c g] [i a] [s n] [e t] _____

4. [p d] [r i] [o s] [f t] [o r] [u i] [n c] [d t] _____

5. [c c] [o o] [m n] [m t] [e i] [r n] [c u] [e e] _____

6. [q p] [u r] [e a] [s c] [t t] [i i] [o c] [n e] _____

Completion time: _____

How well did you do? Now that you have the hang of it, make a prediction for how long it will take you to do the next exercise. Can you better your first score? How long do you think it will take you to do the second exercise? Now record your starting time, set your timer, and get started.

Starting time: _____

1. [i n] [d e] [e w] [n c] [t o] [i m] [f e] [y r] _____
2. [a p] [d r] [e e] [q v] [u i] [a o] [t u] [e s] _____
3. [c s] [o t] [m a] [p n] [u d] [t a] [e r] [r d] _____
4. [e f] [m a] [p m] [l i] [o l] [y i] [e a] [r r] _____
5. [r o] [e u] [g t] [i l] [o y] [n i] [a n] [l g] _____
6. [v m] [i e] [o t] [l a] [e p] [n h] [c o] [e r] _____

Completion time: _____

By the way, you can work with a friend who is also interested in self-challenging activities. Each of you should make five or ten of the exercises and then exchange them with each other. To prepare the exercises, just find words with the same number of letters and write the words side by side, letter by letter, as shown in the exercise.

If you really like challenges, choose words longer than eight letters and make exercises that have more than six entries.

THINKS DIVERGENTLY

O liver Wendell Holmes observed, "Man's mind stretched to a new idea never goes back to its original dimension." Here's a simple example of a mind-stretcher for you, designed to heighten your awareness of the need for divergent thinking.

Look at the following diagram and decide which letter doesn't belong and why:

b	c
d	g

Very often, as we work to solve problems or create new initiatives, we fail to use all the resources available to us. Why is this so? Sometimes we are so blinded by familiar ways of looking at things that we don't see what is right in front of our eyes. And so we neglect possibilities that could make us more efficient. Oh, yes. The correct answer. It's the letter "t." Why? Because the "t" in the diagram is bigger than the other four letters and also because it is not written as a shadow outline and the other four are. If you are like most people, though, you did not even see a "t" in the diagram.

EXERCISE:

Define your thinking style.

We all know a great deal, especially about ourselves. We know what we like—in art, in music, in food, in a friend. We know (are aware of) what we know about our jobs, our capacity to hold those jobs, and what it will take to continue being successful. But many of us don't know what our thinking style is.

Basically, we have one of two orientations—we depend either on the left hemisphere of the brain extensively or on the right. Neither one is good or bad, right or wrong. It's natural and normal to have such a dependency, just as it's accepted without question that some people are right-handed and others are left-handed.

The problem arises when we have to solve a problem that requires the characteristics of the *other* half of the brain, the one we don't usually use. Is it possible to develop the capacity of the nondominant sphere? Absolutely! In fact, the ideal is to become "lateralized"—able to switch to either sphere depending on the parameters of the problem.

Before you can begin to develop your seldom-used side, however, you need to determine which side you're currently using. Here are some true-or-false questions to help you decide that:

_____ 1. I often depend on my intuition.

_____ 2. I have a good vocabulary and good language skills.

_____ 3. I have an efficient filing system.

_____ 4. I make connections (see relationships) fairly easily.

_____ 5. I have a good sense of humor and/or am known as a funny person.

_____ 6. I consider myself (and/or am considered by others) as an emotional person.

_____ 7. I often decide to do things spontaneously.

_____ 8. I have always been good with numbers.

_____ 9. I prefer to read the owner's manual rather than experiment with a new purchase.

_____ 10. I daydream at least once a day.

_____ 11. I prefer the "bird's eye" view to the "worm's eye" view.

_____ 12. I am detail oriented.

_____ 13. I like to have all the facts before I make a decision.

Use the following chart to help you tally your choices. Circle the letter "R" or the letter "L" for each item, depending on the answer (true or false) you gave:

	True	False			True	False
1.	R	L		8.	L	R
2.	L	R		9.	L	R
3.	L	R		10.	R	L
4.	L	R		11.	R	L
5.	R	L		12.	L	R
6.	R	L		13.	L	R
7.	R	L				

- How many "R" answers did you have? _____

- How many "L" answers? _____

If you had approximately the same number for each (a 6/7 combination, for example), you are probably lateralized, which is the ideal orientation. It suggests you are mentally "ambidextrous," capable of using either half of your brain, depending on the nature of the problem to be solved.

A majority of "R" answers indicates a right-brain orientation. You tend to be creative, imaginative, spontaneous. Your problem-solving style depends more on fantasy than on facts. To increase your left-brain skills, develop your organizational and follow-through abilities. Use facts more than you do and increase your ability to set time limits and abide by them. Also, work on improving your verbal capability.

If most of your answers were "L" answers, you possess what is known as the "engineering" mind. You are analytical, logical, organized, detailed. You solve problems pragmatically rather than creatively. And many problems do need to be solved this way. Some problems, however, require a right-brained solution. To increase your capacity to tap into this sphere, use "What if . . . ?" questions frequently. Practice drawing or painting. Learn to play a musical instrument. Try to think holistically rather than narrowly.

EXERCISE:

Engage in mental playfulness.

State a condition in your work environment that you feel could be improved (don't tell how to improve it; just describe the situation):

_____

_____

_____

Now look at the problem above and as you do so, allow other words to pop into your head. Write those words in column A below. They will be your first set of stimuli.

	A	B	C
1.	_____	_____	connoisseur
2.	_____	_____	collop
3.	_____	_____	compartment
4.	_____	_____	contest
5.	_____	_____	castanets
6.	_____	_____	cardinal
7.	_____	_____	collywobbles
8.	_____	_____	congregation
9.	_____	_____	cowboy
10.	_____	_____	crust

	A	B	C
11.	_____	_____	currency
12.	_____	_____	cherub
13.	_____	_____	charisma
14.	_____	_____	circle
15.	_____	_____	conch

Next, open a dictionary and find fifteen different words—any words— on fifteen different pages. (You need *not* restrict yourself to pages from a single letter of the alphabet.) In column B, write down the first word that grabs you, whether or not you know its meaning.

Now look at your problem once again and then immediately look at the words in Columns A, B, and C. Take the words and quickly explore them mentally. One of them probably contains the nugget of a good idea, a way of solving the problem. If you still don't have a clue, give your list to a friend and ask for fifteen more freely-associated words and then re-play with the words.

Keep on doing this until you find a word or word-combination that contains the kernel of a solution. Sooner or later you'll find one that triggers a possibility, one that you previously wouldn't have considered. But you must remain open to those possibilities. If you're not capable of mental "free-falling" in the clouds of uncertainty, you will never see new horizons.

HAS A CHILD'S MIND

From Japan comes the word *shoshin,* which is defined as "a beginner's mind." Having a shoshin mind-set means looking at things anew, much as a child would—not yet having formed rigid mind-sets that limit possibilities. Sometimes experience works against us— it prevents us from taking off on flights of fancy. And without such flights, innovations remain stalled on the tarmac of the mundane.

As observed by Buddhist scholar Shunryu Suzuki, "In the beginner's mind there are many possibilities; in the expert's mind there are few." One technique that will help you view problems from a beginner's perspective is to actually ask a child, or several children if you can, how he or she would solve a given problem. The unfettered perspective, the uncluttered view born of innocence rather than experience, is often what we need to invent new realities.

EXERCISE:

Move beyond the known.

Read this actual letter from an administrative professional in a multinational company. She is thanking colleagues in the corporate office for the seminar they arranged for admins throughout the corporation:

Dear Nora/Christine/Lonnie:

I just wanted to let you know that your hard work paid off. After attending the seminar, I decided I had enough confidence in myself and it was my responsibility to share this information with the other secretaries here.

I held a briefing on Tuesday for all the secretaries (voluntary attendance). The response was overwhelming—14 of 15 secretaries attended.

The presentation was just a brief overview taking one and a half hours. We discussed: Who we are? What we are? Where do we want to be? What can we do about it? (I used all my material from the seminar in Calabasas.) There was plenty of discussion. We could have used the whole day.

I have enclosed a copy of the slides and handouts. (They might be of use to someone else.) Each secretary was also given a company pen, a bound notepad, and a looseleaf book with "My Job—How to do it when I am away" (adapted for our office with all our forms and general information added). These little extras were very well received.

Starting in the new year we will have monthly meetings with pre-selected topics. We are also going to have each Director take a turn at explaining his/her department at the beginning of each meeting. We hope to have training sessions, et cetera.

I would never have imagined that I could do this. Thanks to you, Nora, Christine, and Lonnie, and especially Marlene [the seminar presenter],

68

talking and sharing with all the other secretaries, I did it. (If I had been asked to do this six months ago, I could not have done it. I must admit it was very scary but very worthwhile.)

Many, many thanks to all of you!

"If you always do what you've always done, you'll always be what you've always been."

Barb Hutchinson
(reprinted with permission)

In what specific ways has this individual grown in the short period of six months? _____

_____

_____

_____

_____

_____

Her letter should have given you some ideas of your own. What are they? _____

_____

_____

_____

_____

_____

In your opinion, what is necessary for increasing self-confidence?

_____

_____

_____

_____

_____

Do you wish to "be what you've always been"? _____

If so, why? _____

If not—if you wish to grow beyond your current excellence—explain
why. _____

_____

_____

_____

_____

_____

What benefits might result—for you, for other secretaries, for your
organization—if you move beyond "what you've always done"?

_____

_____

_____

_____

_____

_____

EXERCISE:

Develop worst-case/best-case scenarios.

As adults, we cannot realistically view the world with the same sense of wonder we did as children. We have seen too much, done too much, learned too much. But we can temporarily suspend disbelief and allow ourselves to be caught up in imaginings. As you contemplate your profession, ask if you would want your child to enter it. (Most admins don't.) If not, what are your reasons?

_____

_____

_____

_____

_____

If you *would* want your child to become an administrative professional, what are your reasons?

_____

_____

_____

_____

_____

Now think about the profession ten years from now. What are the best possible conditions associated with that role?

_____

_____

_____

_____.

_____

What is a worst-case scenario for admins ten years hence? (Try not to merely supply the opposite of what you wrote above.)

_____

_____

_____

_____

_____

Experts predict that the administrative function will actually be split in the future—skilled admins will assume more managerial functions. Those who don't continuously update their skills will be relegated to clerical responsibilities.

And so, it seems, it will be both the best of times and the worst of times for admins, depending on how much of a commitment they are willing to make to continuing education.

Having reviewed both your worst-case and your best-case scenario as well, what do you need to do to ensure the latter is more likely to be part of your future?

_____

_____

_____

_____

_____

_____

_____

_____

_____

_____

_____

_____

_____

INTERVIEW:

Nancy Parent, Office Manager for the Department of Research, Evaluation and Testing, City School District, Rochester, New York

Q: Given these traits, which do you feel is most important for administrative professionals and why?

A: Due to the professional atmosphere that most offices try to uphold, a good administrative professional needs many skills and qualities to cope in the business environment. There are many traits that distinguish an exceptional administrative assistant. Essential characteristics that help someone achieve and be successful in this field include the following:

- **Organizational skills** rank high on the list. The ability to refer to prior work to answer questions is needed to function effectively in the workplace. When you are organized, you can find things quickly and efficiently. Organization begins within you, whether you categorize, keep a list or divide work into piles. Finding what works best for you is finding organization.

- **Self-confidence** is important not only on a personal level, but on a professional level as well. If you demonstrate self-doubt, chances are your boss will have less confidence in your ability to perform. Believe in yourself, and you can achieve your goals.

- **Attendance** is one hundred percent imperative. No work can be accomplished if you 're not present. Attendance will lead to dependability. Dependability will lead to a connection with your boss. A connection with your boss can lead to advancements.

- **Lifelong learning** is probably the most important asset anyone can possess. If someone told me in high school that I had to continue to educate myself, I would not have believed that person. Because the world is constantly changing, the ability to engage in your

Secrets of the Frontline Superstars

surroundings and absorb knowledge benefits not only you but also others you may come in contact with. It's similar to the "circle of life." You feed from someone's knowledge and someone feeds from yours. Wisdom can only be acquired if you have an open mind and are able to adapt to a variety of situations.

- **The ability to juggle tasks** is extremely important in today's society. With most homes needing two incomes, the skill of handling the multiple priorities of home, family, and career is essential. Things have to be prioritized and done accordingly.

- **Willingness to explore/original thoughts.** As Bob Dylan said decades ago, "The times they are a-changing." Being able to keep up with the times is critical to career success. Take a quick look back over the innovations of the past few decades, from the original telephone to today's cell phones, from typewriters to computers, and from carbon paper to copy machines. What will the future hold? That future awaits your exploration.

Additional thoughts about the future, hectic office environments, and lessons learned:

"The factory of the future will have only two employees, a man and a dog. The man will be there to feed the dog. The dog will be there to keep the man from touching the equipment."

In my eyes, the man still has the upper hand. The dog is keeping the man from touching the equipment, but without food and nourishment, the dog would become weak. There's a partnership evident here. Similarly, most jobs depend upon other people to complete a task from beginning to end. It is vital to be able to work well with others and develop a sense of camaraderie. Working as a team will make your job easier and will benefit the organization as a whole.

All work environments are hectic at times. Being able to negotiate the stress and still function is a valuable skill. Some people shut down, while others thrive on pressure. If you belong in the former category, acquire some new coping skills.

There are many ways to deal with stress. Prioritize and focus on what needs to be done. Completing one task at a time and moving to the next will help accomplish the day's work. Keeping focused on the task at hand, while handling interruptions, requires organization. In a busy, stressful, hectic job, the need for organization is imperative.

Having worked in offices for twenty-seven years, I've seen the value of organization over and over again. I have learned a number of key ideas to improve my performance at my job. Many different people have inspired me in many different ways. One thing I have learned that has brought me wisdom is to listen. Some people just hear, but the people who can listen will optimize what is being said.

ESCAPES MENTAL RESTRAINTS

"All behavior consists of opposites ... Learn to see things backward, inside out, and upside down." Lao-tzu's statement is strong encouragement for you to think in ways that aren't natural or normal. Mind-stretching takes some work—especially at first—for it requires leaving the security of traditional mental moorings. But the creative mind is meant to pioneer, to escape the familiar and explore the unknown.

EXERCISE:

Discover your assumptions and then work without them.

We sometimes create shadows that prevent the light of discovery from shining through. These shadows are self-imposed limits: We often assume restraints when none exist. The following five-minute experiment illustrates this point.

If possible, work at your desk—either at home or at the office. Have a timer ready and set it for five minutes as soon as you understand the directions that follow: You are to create as many sentences as you possibly can in a five-minute period. The sentences can have only five words. The first word in every sentence must begin with the letter "A." The second word in every sentence must begin with the letter "B." The third word in every sentence must begin with the letter "C." The fourth word in every sentence must begin with the letter "D." And the last word in every sentence must begin with the letter "E." Once you have used a word, you cannot use it again.

Here are some examples: A   B   C   D   E

All beasts can dance effortlessly.

Another boy could design everything.

1. _____

2. _____

3. _____

4. _____

5. _____

6. _____

7. _____

8. _____

9. _____

10. _____

11. _____

12. _____

13. _____

14. _____

15. _____

16. _____

17. _____

18. _____

19. _____

20. _____

How did you do? Most people are able to generate five to eight sentences. (If you got as many as twenty, you are among a very rare group.) Now let's examine some assumptions. Did you assume at first that you couldn't use a dictionary? Did you actually use a dictionary? Those who wind up with a high number of sentences usually realize they aren't breaking any rules by using available resources.

Did you assume the sentences had to be "built" horizontally? Did you create horizontal or vertical sentences? Would you have been able to create more sentences if you had listed twenty "A" words, then twenty beginning with "B," and so on?

Did you assume you couldn't use proper nouns? Did you actually use them? Perhaps you could have created more sentences if you had done the task in the following way. Try it, and see whether you come up with more sentences.

First, create a column of nouns or adjectives starting with the letter "A." Once that column is complete, write twenty "B" words—verbs if you started with nouns, and nouns if you started with adjectives. In the third column, write "C" words—nouns if you started with nouns and verbs if you started with adjectives. Your fourth column will contain all "D" words and the final column, all "E" words.

As you attack problems in the future, arm yourself with as many tools as you can. One of the most effective tools is the ability to challenge or suspend your assumptions.

EXERCISE:

Personify your problems.

This technique taps into our infinite capacity for imagination. Caution: If you have never tried this before, you may find it difficult to slip into the territory of the imagination. There are no signposts here. Cartographers have prepared no maps. When you work with methods like this, you are exploring unfamiliar "terra," which will not become "firma" until you have returned to it several times.

1. Write down a problem you (or your organization) are facing now or will have to face in the future: _____

   _____

   _____

   _____

2. Now imagine that your problem is actually a person, a person from another time, another place. Personify your problem. Pretend that it's someone living in a different era, a different city. What sort of person do you see in your mind's eye right now? _____

   _____

   _____

3. Now list the traits/qualities/characteristics/behaviors/visuals/ entities associated with that person. For example, if the problem you described in #1 were reduced budgets causing reduced training opportunities, you might view this problem as a dentist in an ultra-modern office. The aspects/items associated with such an individual could be Novocaine and listening to soothing music.

These two characteristics alone could spark partial solutions for your problem. For example, what might lessen the pain of having fewer training opportunities? Possibly having skilled employees (instead of outside instructors) train others in informal settings. For the selected individuals, the recognition they receive would certainly soften the blow of not attending formal classes. Listening to music might make you think of audiotapes. For a minimal fee, the company could invest in audiotapes of the leading business books. Discussion groups could subsequently be formed.

Go on now to list the traits/qualities/characteristics/behaviors/visuals/entities associated with your problem. Choose any persona except the dentist illustrated here and the sheriff used as an example in #4.

_____   _____   _____

_____   _____   _____

_____   _____   _____

4. Now see yourself solving the problem as that person would solve the problem. To illustrate, say that you personified the problem as a sheriff in the Old West. In that era, sheriffs often formed posses. One possible solution to your problem, then, might be to join forces with a number of other people. ("There's strength in numbers.") Sheriffs wear badges, showing the law is on their side. Another possible solution to your problem could be legal precedents that would lend weight to the proposal or cause you are pursuing.

What aspects of your personified figure (your problem in disguise) might help solve this current problem? Look back to the traits you listed in #3, let your mind wander, think again about the two examples, and then explore possible solutions based on the features possessed by the persona you have chosen to represent your problem. _____

_____

_____

SEES THE BIG PICTURE

W e sometimes become so immersed in the nitty-gritty that we fail to remember why we're doing the nitty-gritty to begin with. "What larger purpose is this activity serving?" is a question you should ask yourself several times each day. If there's no important bigger purpose, or if the activity doesn't relate directly to the organizational mission or your personal goals, reexamine its necessity.

EXERCISE:

Ask questions.

No matter how independent we think we are, we cannot work in isolation. Your work affects the work of other people. And the work of other people influences the work you do.

A. List the names of three people you depend on to do the work you're expected to do:

1. _____

2. _____

3. _____

B. Now list the names of three people who depend on you to do the work they're expected to do:

1. _____

2. _____

3. _____

C. If one of the people you listed asked you one of the following questions, how would you respond? Write your answers in the blanks.

- What benefits our customers most? _____

_____

_____

_____

- What is wasting time? _____

_____

_____

- What doesn't need to be done? _____

_____

_____

- What is most important to the mission? _____

_____

_____

- What could I do to make your job easier? _____

_____

_____

- Other questions? _____

_____

_____

D. Take the initiative to meet informally with one person whose work affects your own and with another person who depends on you. Ask each other the questions in Section C. What innovations or improvements might result from such a meeting?

_____

_____

_____

_____

_____

EXERCISE:

Look for resources from within.

You know yourself well, but you probably don't really know the heights you're capable of reaching. The life of the average administrative professional is a busy one—both inside and outside the office. As a result, there's little time for introspection. Typically, we don't plumb our inner depths unless we're forced to. Try the following exercise to get a handle on who you think you are.

A. As quickly as you can, jot down ten adjectives to describe yourself. Use words that reflect attitudes, emotions, and capability rather than ones that describe physical traits ("intelligent" rather than "tall" for example). Write the first ten that pop into your head:

1. _____

2. _____

3. _____

4. _____

5. _____

6. _____

7. _____

8. _____

9. _____

10. _____

Secrets of the Frontline Superstars

Did you find it difficult to describe yourself? Most people do. Even though you have lived with yourself for twenty or thirty years or more, you may not ever have assessed yourself in this way. One interesting experiment is to ask others who know you well to write down ten nonphysical adjectives that describe you. Compare the list and analyze the discrepancies.

Others no doubt will see things in you that you don't see in yourself. And there will be those who fail to see some things that you might feel are the essential you. As the ancient Greeks told us, "The unexamined life is not worth living." Periodically examine yourself and your life so that you can enjoy both more fully.

As you complete the second half of this exercise, *don't look* at the list of adjectives you just jotted down on the preceding page.

B.   Now create a list of ten nonphysical adjectives that describe you—the first ten that pop into your head—but this time, write with your opposite hand!

1. _____

2. _____

3. _____

4. _____

5. _____

6. _____

7. _____

8. _____

9. _____

10. _____

Compare your two lists now. In theory, they should be the same—you wrote about the same subject—one you know very well—and you made the second list just minutes after composing the first. The only difference was that you switched the pen from one hand to the other. (The lists are seldom identical.)

What did you learn about yourself? _____

_____

_____

_____

_____

_____

_____

_____

COPES WITH REJECTION

S uccess seldom comes to those unwilling to progress beyond their first failure. It's the ability to withstand rejection that separates successful dreamers from unsuccessful ones. If you have a good idea, you must protect it from outside forces that could easily destroy it. If you have faith in your abilities, you must make yourself less vulnerable to criticism.

Be encouraged by three guests who once appeared on a television talk show. All three were self-made millionaires by their mid-thirties. They had one thing in common—they averaged eighteen failures in nonsuccessful ventures before they finally met with success. Use such stories to buoy your spirits when support for your idea is disappearing.

Helen Keller certainly possessed the ability to regard setbacks as successes lurking incognito: "When one door of opportunity closes, another opens; but often we look so long at the closed door that we do not see the one which has been opened for us."

As thinking people, we always have choices. We can choose to remain mired in current failure or we can rise above it to head toward future achievements. It is fairly easy to complain—particularly if the past grievance was undeserved. It is harder to do something constructive about the complaint, to move on to a solution instead of remaining in the bog of accusation. Which sort of person are you? Do you savor the flavor of despair? Or do you prefer turning "lemons" into metaphorical "lemonade"?

EXERCISE:

Find a "failure hero" and let that person be your guide.

Can you identify this person?

When he was 22, his business failed.

When he was 23, he was defeated in his bid for the legislature.

When he was 24, he experienced another business failure.

When he was 25, he was successful in his efforts to be elected to the legislature.

When he was 26, the woman he loved died.

When he was 27, he suffered a nervous breakdown.

When he was 29, he was denied a chance to be a speaker.

When he was 31, he lost a bid to be an elector.

When he was 34, he ran for Congress and was defeated.

When he was 37, he was successful in running for Congress.

When he was 39, he mounted an unsuccessful campaign for Congress.

When he was 46, he was defeated in his efforts to become a senator.

When he was 47, he experienced failure in his vice-presidential efforts.

When he was 49, he was defeated in his attempt to become a senator.

When he was 51, he was chosen to be President of the United States of America.

This remarkably persistent person was Abraham Lincoln, a true "failure hero." Find another—perhaps by interviewing someone in your own organization—and write that person's record in a manner similar to the one above. Keep that record posted and turn to it for inspiration.

EXERCISE:

Test your "flopportunity" quotient.

This simple test will give you an indication of your willingness to let a setback turn into a flop or into an opportunity. If you are easily discouraged, if mistakes make you feel unworthy, if you cannot see beyond today's darkness into tomorrow's sunlight—then the opportunity will disintegrate and the temporary failure will assume an importance it doesn't deserve.

On the other hand, if you can persevere, if you can view rejection as a step in the path of success, if you really can train yourself to hope eternally, then quite possibly the flop will become an opportunity.

Check the blank ("Yes" or "No") that best reflects your response to each question. Be as honest with yourself as possible—no one else will see your answers.

Yes _____ No _____ 1. Little things tend to upset me.

Yes _____ No _____ 2. I have an extensive support network.

Yes _____ No _____ 3. I enjoy hearing success stories, especially if they began in adversity.

Yes _____ No _____ 4. I believe in self-indulgence on occasion.

Yes _____ No _____ 5. I would define myself as a pessimist.

Yes _____ No _____ 6. I remember to appreciate each day.

Yes _____ No _____ 7. I can shut out negative thoughts.

Yes _____ No _____ 8. I believe most clouds have silver linings.

Yes _____ No _____ 9. I equate failure with humiliation.

Yes _____ No _____ 10. I believe I have control over my life.

Yes _____ No _____ 11. I usually depend on others to effect change.

Yes _____ No _____ 12. I feel fortunate to be/have what I am/have.

Yes _____ No _____ 13. I tend to envy the circumstances of others.

Score your responses using this chart.

  1. "yes," -10 points; "no," +10 points

  2. "yes," +10 points; "no," -10 points

  3. "yes," +10 points; "no," -10 points

  4. "yes," +10 points; "no," -10 points

  5. "yes," -10 points; "no," +10 points

  6. "yes," +10 points; "no," -10 points

  7. "yes," +10 points; "no," -10 points

  8. "yes," +10 points; "no," -10 points

  9. "yes," -10 points; "no," +10 points

10. "yes," +10 points; "no," -10 points

11. "yes," -10 points; "no," +10 points

12. "yes," +10 points; "no," -10 points

13. "yes," -10 points; "no," +10 points

If you scored 80+ points, there's a very strong possibility that you can convert flops to "ops." You are realistic enough to know that while every cloud may have a silver lining, the very existence of clouds means some rain will fall into your life. But you are aware of choices—you can either be drenched by the deluge or can splash about a bit and then go indoors to get warm.

If you scored below 80, you may wish to take stock of the many blessings you have. And look back over the times of adversity and remind yourself of how much better you are for having experienced them.

Is
PERSISTENT

Perseverance has been defined as the "eternal try-angle." How would you define it? Perhaps more important, do you agree with the definition of a "try-angle"? When life knocks you down—and it will—have you the courage and persistance to get right back up? Administrative professionals who have good ideas that aren't initially accepted know they can either abandon the idea or resubmit it. Losers give up; winners keep on trying. Eventually, with enough trys and even trials, the idea will gain acceptance. (Even if it does not, you will be admired for your "do-or-die" attitude.) Creative ideas need you to fight on their behalf. Be an idea-warrior, knowing that you won't win every battle but you will win the war, the war against complacency.

EXERCISE:

Gauge your ability to persevere rather than perseverate.

There is a distinction between persevering and perseverating. And a very simple experiment will tell you which you are more inclined to do. From the following sentence, one letter of the alphabet has been removed—from 11 places in the sentence. You can probably figure out the missing letter fairly quickly. But can you figure out the sentence?

VRYVNINGLLNATSLDRBRRYPI.

When you have finished, review your thinking process and answer these questions:

1. What word did you begin with? _____

    _____

    _____

2. If you began with the word "very," approximately how long did you stay with it? _____

    _____

    _____

3. Did you feel frustrated when you could not get it to "fit" into the rest of the sentence? _____

    _____

    _____

Secrets of the Frontline Superstars

4. Were you annoyed or challenged by the prospect of finding another first word? _____

_____

_____

_____

5. If you began with the word "every," how long did it take you to realize you were on the right track? _____

_____

_____

_____

6. Did you look at the whole line first, trying to figure out individual words, or did you start at the beginning and try to figure out individual words? _____

_____

_____

_____

The sentence, of course, is "Every evening Ellen eats elderberry pie." Although the missing letter "e" may have been obvious to you, you probably had to make several efforts to learn where the words divided. People who "perseverate" continue a behavior even if the desired effect is not being achieved. Those who "persevere" do not engage in repetitive behavior unless it is leading them to a goal. Clearly, it is better to persevere, to have the stick-to-it-ive-ness that helps us ultimately achieve the goals we have set for ourselves.

EXERCISE:

Use several "doors" to gain entry.

"Don't argue about difficulties. The difficulties will argue for themselves." The words of Winston Churchill apply equally well to individuals or teams. We often allow problems to assume the driver's seat and lead us to dead ends. We focus so intensively on the negative that we don't give positives a chance to be seen or heard.

Creative employees, by contrast, know that if obvious answers aren't attainable, there are less-obvious answers that may serve as well or nearly as well. If the front door doesn't allow access to the solution, they will try other doors and even windows to gain entry.

To illustrate, assume your dream is to play in the National Basketball Association (NBA). But your size and your sex make that dream impossible to attain. Rather than closing the door on the NBA-nexus, you might consider a related job. There are no doubt more than you realized:

Coach	Director of Publications and Information
Assistant Coach	Video Coordinator
Business Manager	Scout
Director of Marketing	Team Physician
Director of Administration	Strength and Conditioning Coach
Director of Community Relations	Trainer
Director of Scouting Services	Assistant Trainer
Director of Public Relations	Executive Director
Basketball Consultant	Manager of Community Programs
Choreographer	Manager of Cheerleaders
Cheerleader	Manager of Promotions

Now, write down one of your goals: _____

_____

_____

_____

_____

_____

_____

What obstacles are keeping you from that goal? _____

_____

_____

_____

_____

_____

What other doors could you walk through in order to achieve that goal?

_____

_____

_____

_____

_____

_____

_____

Is
SELF-CONFIDENT

W e all have good ideas. Some of us, though, are more willing to fight for them than others are. Think about the last good idea you had. What happened to it? What *typically* happens to your ideas?

Often, ideas are born of faith and need faith to sustain them until they reach maturity. After all, the Wright brothers only *thought* their plane would fly—they had no proof. And so it goes with discoveries both physical and cerebral—if not for the confidence the idea-proposer has in him- or herself and in the capacity of others to follow through, good ideas might only be fleeting thoughts.

EXERCISE:

Prepare a "birth" announcement.

Imagine you have been asked to write a birth announcement (or a "worth" announcement) for a good idea you or your team recently had. By publicly proclaiming a well-researched proposal, you can often garner support that helps you sustain the faith you have in the innovation.

You may use the accompanying form or one that you create yourself. Either way, the form should serve as a succinct means of advising others of your efforts to continuously bring improvement. In fact, you may wish to mention that you're working on such a form and would like to share it with them in the future in order to facilitate communication. Then, when you've done your homework, simply fill out the form and distribute it.

Announcing

Idea: _____

_____

Cost: _____

_____

Benefits: _____

_____

Precedents: _____

_____

Who will be affected: _____

_____

Approval required: _____

_____

When to start: _____

_____

Comments: _____

_____

Submitted by: _____ *Date:* _____

EXERCISE:

Keep a log to chart the progress of your ideas.

Records can help you understand what went wrong and what went right with the ideas you propose. Your charting need not be complex (it can be as simple as the sample Idea Tracker on the next page), but it should help you trace the history of your innovative proposals so you can learn which stumbling blocks may have destroyed the confidence you initially felt in your idea. Begin with your most recent good idea.

IDEA TRACKER

Idea: _____

Date: _____

Efforts I made to implement it: _____

_____

_____

Results of those efforts: _____

_____

_____

What I learned that will be useful next time:

_____

_____

What I will avoid next time: _____

_____

_____

INTERVIEW:

Amelia Barclay, former International President of the International Association of Administrative Professionals (IAAP).

Q: *Given these traits, which do you feel is most important for administrative professionals and why?*

A: Self-direction is critically important because in today's business setting, the administrative professional is expected to work more independently. The executive she serves is too occupied with big-picture tasks and responsibilities to be available for constant direction, advice, and guidance. Additionally, he or she may be away from the office much of the time, traveling to meetings, entertaining clients, etc. The role of the administrative professional is evolving increasingly to that of office manager. This evolution represents a golden opportunity for the administrative professional to demonstrate the ability to accept additional responsibility.

Q: *How did you handle the stress associated with your job?*

A: During my 45-year administrative professional career, I encountered only two stressful episodes. The hardest was adjusting to the temperament of the university president with whom I worked for 28 years. A lawyer by profession, he enjoyed arguing—just for fun!

I was more reserved in temperament and had great difficulty adjusting to his management style. He didn't relish peace, preferring a more lively office atmosphere. Once I learned to respond in kind to his bent for sparring (colleagues told us we should be on the stage!), we established a unique working relationship that led to a lively, never-dull sojourn.

Q: *It's been said that results depend on relationships. What suggestions to you have for optimizing one's relationship with one's manager and other key players at work?*

A: • It's important for the manager/administrative assistant team to learn the other person's personality style as it relates to communication, likes, dislikes, reactions to situations in the office, etc. Really getting to know a person is the key to optimizing any relationship. Outgoing personalities afford easier and quicker access than reticent ones, who require more effort to assess their inner thoughts and feelings. But it is worth the effort, to reach common ground and establish a relationship based on understanding "where the person is coming from."

Q: *What macrocosmic challenges facing the nation may be microcosmically affecting the way today's administrative professional work?*

A: • The state of the economy is a constant concern for all of corporate America. Its basic unpredictability from day to day affects everyone. Downsizing is rampant, leading to considerable uneasiness in the workplace, especially at the administrative professional job level. The war in Iraq affects every American, economically and emotionally. The high price of gasoline is only one example of its effect. The division of opinion about being at war may cause conflict in the office itself.

Q: *The only constant, it seems, is change. In some organizations, in fact, the descriptive sentence is "No sooner said … than changed!" What can administrative professionals do to accept—perhaps even embrace—change?*

A: The fact that we are all affected by constant change affords us the opportunity to realize that everyone is in this together. Small comfort, perhaps, but a starting point for accepting the inevitable and adapting as best we can under the circumstances. Actually, we are already well acquainted with change, having handled it progressively over the years. From the inception of technological advances, front-line professionals have been the ones to meet the learning challenges head-on and set the example for management when their turn came to adapt to change.

Q: *What "lessons learned" can you share with others on how to be a "frontline superstar"?*

A: Realize that your executive needs you to "run interference" for him or her. Become adept at fielding calls and screening visitors, to free him or her for major tasks. Learn your manager's style and emulate it as appropriate in representing him/her to other employees. Accommodate yourself to his/her habits and idiosyncrasies—they are not going to change. Protect confidences. Your manager will need to share with you information that must be kept within the confines of the office. As the one who works most closely with him or her, the value of your trustworthiness in this regard is priceless.

Q: *What advice can you give regarding updating one's skills?*

A: Keeping current with administrative skills is a constant priority. Computer technology changes almost daily, it seems, and there is no substitute for keeping current with these changes. Most companies, I would think, make provision for required training through both internal and external programs. If yours does not, inquire having training offered. Clearly, the company will reap the rewards of such training. Usually, the astute executive is well aware of the advantages and benefits of having administrative professionals keep their skills updated. However, if these opportunities are not available to you, you would be wise to pursue them on your own.

Is
PATIENT
WITH IDEAS

Yes, it is possible to be spontaneously imaginative—to spin off a dozen ideas in the blink of an eye. It's also possible to let your subconscious grapple with a problem over a period of hours or days or even weeks. When you let your ideas "incubate," you usually produce more sophisticated ones that become solutions to more complex problems. Let your subconscious go to work for you. At night, before you retire, think about a problem you're facing or a situation you'd like to make better. During your sleeping hours, your subconscious will actually wrestle with the problem and, in time, will find an answer.

EXERCISE:

Immunize yourself against "imagicides."

There will always be those who, deliberately or inadvertently, will engage in "imagicide"—they will attempt to "kill your imaginings," to strangle your good ideas.

You've heard these killer phrases—perhaps you've even used some yourself:

"Just do your work. We don't pay you to think."

"We've tried it before."

"It'll never work."

"Management will never approve it."

"It costs too much."

"That's a dumb idea."

Your idea, in a sense, owes its life to you. But you have some responsibility too. A parent gives birth but cannot subsequently abandon the child. Similarly, once you have given birth to a good idea, you are expected to sustain it, to give it life—at least until you reach the point where you must give the idea a proper burial. But give it time to incubate and grow first.

How can you immunize yourself during the gestation period?

- **Anticipate "imagicides."** Make yourself mentally ready for the comments you are bound to hear and tell yourself you are strong enough to withstand any and all of them.

- **Keep a diary of successful ideas you've proposed in the past.**
  You don't need to memorize this material, but "know" what's on it so
  you can offer concrete examples of past success to offset the force of
  future criticism.

- **Ask a question of the idea-slayer.** For example, "Why don't you
  think it will work?" "What would you propose instead?" "Did you
  forget that management is actively seeking our ideas?"

- **Ask to implement the idea for a trial period.** If you have paved
  the way sufficiently, the idea should enjoy some measure of success.
  You can then ask to extend the trial period to make the idea standard
  operating procedure.

- **Obtain the support of someone in the organization who is well
  respected.** When appropriate, let others know you have the
  endorsement of someone in management.

- **Find precedents, either in your organization's history or in the
  history of comparable organizations.** People are more willing to try
  new ideas if they know those ideas have been tried in other places.

- **Make certain you've played devil's advocate with your own
  idea.** Be prepared to defend it by deflecting the negative comments.
  Be certain, too, to have at your fingertips persuasive facts and figures
  that present the benefits that will accrue if your idea is adopted.

Like parenthood, self-defense and idea defense are not easy. But the
maturing of the seeds into fruit is well worth the effort.

EXERCISE:

Create a climate conducive to incubation.

What happens to a good idea immediately after it's popped into your head? What's the climate you've created for sustaining it? Complete the following sentences to make you more aware of the mental environment in which your imaginings thrive or expire. Place an "X" beside the response in the middle or right-hand column, whichever most resembles the reality of your life.

1. My work space is like	☐ a monastery	☐ a kindergarten
2. My verbal style is like	☐ a librarian's	☐ a circus performer's
3. My documentation is like	☐ a bank	☐ a jazz score written on a paper napkin
4. My thinking style is like	☐ a Japanese garden	☐ Disneyworld
5. My concentration ability is like	☐ hopscotch	☐ Ping-Pong
6. My perseverance is like	☐ a hothouse flower	☐ a weed
7. My self-confidence is like	☐ air	☐ concrete
8. My personality is like	☐ skiing	☐ stamp collecting
9. My goals are like	☐ a kitten	☐ a tiger
10. My attitude toward life is like	☐ Sunday school	☐ a martial arts class

11. My willingness to stand up for myself is like ☐ the Constitution ☐ a handshake

12. My non-work life is like ☐ a dream ☐ a nightmare

13. My creative ability is like ☐ summer vacation ☐ the Christmas holidays

14. My communication style is like ☐ Abraham Lincoln ☐ W.C. Fields

15. My decision-making style is like ☐ pin the tail on the donkey ☐ a love sonnet

Only you can interpret what your forced-choice answers mean. As you review your "X" choices, describe the general environments—both interior and exterior—that are part of your life:

_____

_____

_____

_____

_____

_____

_____

_____

_____

_____

Finally, answer these questions about your environments and the ideas that are born in them.

1. As you think about your interior environment, would you agree it contains the serenity required for ideas to incubate? _____
If "yes," what good ideas have "hatched" lately as the result of quiet and perhaps even subconscious incubation?

_____

_____

_____

If "no," what can you do to de-stress your mind? _____

_____

_____

2. As you think about your exterior environment, would you agree it is both organized and yet stimulating so ideas can percolate without danger of evaporating?_____ If "yes," what parts of your work environment do you feel are most beneficial to idea-incubation? How can you increase or enhance those areas?

_____

_____

If "no," ask a colleague's advice on how to organize your workstation better and yet keep it appealing and interesting. Record the advice below.

_____

_____

_____

_____

Is
RESOURCEFUL

The imaginative employee avoids wailing and hand wringing. Instead of complaining about resources that aren't available, the resourceful individual uses what is available and uses it well. Necessity, after all, is the mother of invention. As William McGowan, founder of MCI Communications, wisely commented: "Significant progress doesn't come from the formal planning process of an American corporation. It comes from a couple of guys doing something that hasn't been set down on a list."

There is much to be said for formality—of planning processes and other structured, proven techniques. However, the organization that understands the haphazardness of spontaneous creativity knows that good ideas can come at any time, in any place, to anyone.

EXERCISE:

Look within and without.

In a famous experiment involving resourcefulness, students in an engineering class at a major university were given this assignment (can you figure it out?):

The students were given one hour to remove two Ping-Pong balls from the bottom of a narrow metal cylinder that had been bolted to the floor of their science lab. They could not leave the classroom (to obtain a vacuum cleaner, for example), but they were free to use anything in the lab (such as bubblegum they might have been chewing).

The engineering students failed to find a solution—even though it was right in front of them all along: They could have filled the cylinder with water and the Ping-Ping balls would have *floated* to the top. Water was in the room; likewise talents are within each employee. If the water isn't noticed, it won't be turned on.

But if bosses aren't able to see or discover the inner resources employees have, and/or if employees aren't able to assess their own strengths, the resources will not be used. With that in mind, answer the following questions to identify the "resources" that are within you. Good ideas are truly all around us and within us!

What do you feel is the greatest contribution you can make to
your organization? _____

_____

_____

_____

When is the last time someone asked you the above question? _____

_____

_____

What would your boss say is the greatest contribution you can make or
are making to the organization? _____

_____

_____

_____

_____

Would you be willing to ask your boss this question and then to see how
closely his or her answer matches your own? _____

_____

_____

_____

_____

In every organization, valuable resources, including human resources,
are overlooked and underused. But you can change that reality with a
modicum of effort.

EXERCISE:

Establish communities to broaden your resources.

Administrative professionals who want to make a difference know the process is facilitated when people work together. Witness EAGLES—an Empowered Action Group Leading and Excelling in Support, a group from the Franciscan Health System of Cincinnati, Inc. It began when a Quality Action Team asked them to "meet on a regular basis to establish procedures and to create an atmosphere for coordinating and standardizing management support functions by promoting communication, teamwork, and empowerment."

These five support staff members, in addition to their regular work, participated in a number of activities, including the quarterly publication of the *EAGLES Express*. In the very first issue were articles about empowerment, surveys, and available courses, as well as information about equipment and about a local grammar hotline. The EAGLES established both micro and macro communities within their organization in an effort to improve quality and productivity.

Think about your own organization as a pie. What core values represent the cohesive crust? To what beliefs about the organization do virtually all employees subscribe? _____

_____

_____

_____

_____

_____

Divide up this organizational pie into the major departments or functions of your workplace:

Which departments could you form an alliance with to improve processes and/or products? Place an "A" in that slice of the pie. Work within your professional community to find alliance members.

Is ENTREPRENEURIAL

A chievement is a vital aspect of the entrepreneurial spirit. Setting one's own challenges and experiencing the thrill of victory or the agony of defeat—on an individual basis—drive the entrepreneur. The innovative administrative professional is not "Stepford secretary." (*The Stepford Wives* was a novel by Ira Levin in which women were made into automatons so they could become perfect wives.) Certainly, a capable admin will do what is asked, but at the same time continuously try to improve the existing and perhaps even challenge the established. In spirit, the creative admin responds to the Tom Peters' declaration: "The only way you can fail these days is not to try stuff."

Creativity drives the most successful people. They "try stuff." And when the stuff doesn't succeed, they try new stuff, again and again, until they realize their goals.

EXERCISE:

Assess Yourself.

For each item, place an "X" in the column that best represents where you are in terms of independent thought or adventurous spirit:

1. ☐ Need to have exact details on how to do things
   ☐ No real preference
   ☐ Prefer to figure things out for myself

2. ☐ Never contradict
   ☐ In the middle
   ☐ Will speak up as necessary

3. ☐ Like to "paint by number"
   ☐ No real preference
   ☐ Prefer to make my own creations

4. ☐ Like to visit favorite places
   ☐ No real preference
   ☐ Prefer to visit places I have never been

5. ☐ Like to imitate the success of others
   ☐ No real preference
   ☐ Prefer to have others imitate my successes

6. ☐ Enjoy being able to depend on others
   ☐ No real preference
   ☐ Prefer to be independent

7. ☐ Would like to to marry a millionaire
   ☐ Either would be fine
   ☐ Prefer to earn $1 million on my own

8. ☐ Read the end of a mystery first
   ☐ Do both
   ☐ Prefer to figure it out instead of peeking

9. ☐ Buy things (food, clothes, jewelry, cards)
   ☐ No real preference
   ☐ Prefer to make things

10. ☐ Feel comfortable with limited choices
    ☐ No real preference
    ☐ Prefer to consider multiple choices

There are no right or wrong, good or bad answers here. The only question is this: How mentally independent do you wish to be? If you wish to view yourself as mentally independent (and you need such a descriptor if you are to generate novel ideas), then the majority of your "X's" should be in the right-hand column. If you do wish to be regarded as having this entrepreneurial spirit but a majority of your answers fell in the left-hand column, then you need to develop self-confidence through self-challenges.

Try:

- **Engaging in small projects with limited liability.** Offer ideas that have few negative or minor negative consequences. As you gain confidence, you can propose possibilities that will have greater benefits and (usually) greater attendant risks.

- **Asking for new projects.** Suggest, for a change, that the boss allow you to figure out the best way to do a project. If the outcome of the project isn't as good as he or she had expected, you can revert back to the usual process of the boss directing and you following. If you are already at this stage, move on to the next—ask for new assignments instead of waiting for them to be given to you.

- **Logging your accomplishments.** Keep a small notebook to track the success of your entrepreneurial efforts. Ideally, you will have many more successes than failures. Use the successes to remind you of your competence whenever you are in a situation that calls for innovation; use the failures to remind you of the lessons you've learned.

- **Generating multiple options.** Train yourself to avoid "either/or" choices. Instead, offer yourself multiple options and choose the best from a wide array.

- **Brainstorming.** Employ brainstorming or mindmapping (visual free association) frequently to unlock the ideas waiting to spring forth.

- **Obtaining feedback.** Self-opinion is one way to assess the worth of ideas—either in the embryonic stage or in the innovation/ implementation stage. But the opinions of others can also be a valuable source of evaluation and information. Add one person a month to your feedback circle.

EXERCISE:

Dare to do.

Here is a list of activities administrative professionals can easily initiate to improve the workplace. Check one and then describe what you would do to make this entrepreneurial effort a success. Of course, if you'd rather undertake a project that's not listed here, go right ahead.

My choice:

☐ Attend a seminar and share information with others afterward

☐ Plan a special event for Administrative Professionals Week

☐ Create a directory that lists the special expertises of various admins in your organization

☐ Put out a manual for newly hired employees

☐ Offer to teach a course for other admins

☐ Publish a newsletter just for support staff

☐ Establish (or improve) the company library

☐ Plan a multicultural event to highlight the diversity in your workplace

☐ Make a presentation at a conference

☐ Write an article for a magazine

☐ Form a community alliance in your organization

☐ Initiate a recycling effort

☐ Plan a conference for support staff

☐ Have an office-wide or organization-wide "Clean-out-the-Files" day

☐ Benchmark with admins in other organizations

☐ Other _____

_____

_____

_____

To make this project successful, I will have to: _____

_____

_____

_____

_____

_____

_____

_____

DISLIKES ROUTINE

There are people (thank goodness) who enjoy routine work. They take comfort in the familiarity and the predictability of the work expected of them. They like the unchanging repetition of their tasks and take pleasure in the perfunctory nature of their responsibilities.

Others, though, prefer work that is varied. They dislike routine and thrive instead on having "no two days alike." They aren't disturbed by the irregular pattern of their days. Indeed, they find the kaleidoscopic nature of their work exciting. There are people who truly do work well under pressure. They feel exhilarated when phones ring and co-workers or customers stop by—each ring and each visitor with a new piece of that day's jigsaw puzzle, perhaps a new opportunity or an unexpected solution to a problem.

The willingness to welcome the unpredicted is what separates the innovative admin from the merely competent one.

EXERCISE:

Be challenged by chaos.

When you look at the following picture, you probably begin to feel sensory overload. It is extremely "busy"—with many visual images competing for your attention. The chaos, however, can produce a fount of novel thought. As you study this collage, allow your mind to wander and allow the images to impinge upon your consciousness. Let the graphic stimuli wash over you as you think about some contribution you could make to your profession. Do not fear "weird" ideas. (Tom Peters recommends having at least one "weirdo" on staff!) The purpose of this exercise is to practice finding creative ideas in the midst of daily chaos.

In terms of contributions you could make to your profession, what new thoughts did the images on the preceding page inspire in you?

_____

_____

_____

_____

_____

_____

_____

_____

_____

_____

_____

_____

_____

_____

_____

_____

_____

_____

_____

_____

_____

_____

What additional "weird" thoughts have you had regarding your work or your profession? Which of those could be "tamed" into a workable idea? _____

_____

_____

_____

_____

_____

_____

_____

_____

_____

_____

_____

_____

_____

_____

_____

_____

_____

_____

EXERCISE:

Apply the 80/20 rule.

"When you are through changing," someone once observed, "you're through." Imaginative admins offer living examples of lifelong learning. They continuously assess what they're doing in order to maximize results. They constantly look for ways to improve so that waste can be minimized. They automatically consider how work is done so efforts can be optimized.

One specific technique that often helps identify duplication or non-value-added work is called the "80/20 rule." Quite simply, it states that 20 percent of the contributing factors yield 80 percent of the result. For example, if you are a salesperson with ten accounts, two of those accounts will produce the majority (about 80 percent) of your income. These two accounts—referred to as the "vital few"— should receive most of your attention. But often, the novice will divide his or her time equally among the ten accounts—despite the fact that some have a much greater return than others.

A. To determine the "vital few" and the "trivial many" in terms of your work responsibilities, list here all the tasks you are expected to complete in a given week. In other words, what does your job entail? What do you do all day long?

   1. _____

   2. _____

   3. _____

   4. _____

   5. _____

   6. _____

   7. _____

8. _____

9. _____

10. _____

11. _____

12. _____

13. _____

14. _____

15. _____

16. _____

17. _____

18. _____

19. _____

20. _____

B. As you look over your list, identify the three tasks that you consider most important and/or that your boss would view as the most vital and/or that the head of the organization would regard as most supportive of the mission.

1. _____

2. _____

3. _____

C. Approximately how much of your time do you spend on these three things?

D. As you look over the "trivial many," which of them could be

• Eliminated? _____

_____

134

- Streamlined? _____

  _____

- Combined? _____

  _____

- Redesigned? _____

  _____

- Delegated? _____

  _____

- Traded off? _____

  _____

- Modified? _____

  _____

- Performed less often? _____

  _____

- Performed less thoroughly? _____

  _____

- Made a shared responsibility? _____

  _____

Consider what Mary DeVito, Administrative Assistant for Long Term Care at Park Ridge Hospital (in Greece, New York) was able to accomplish by asking some of these very questions:

- To reduce the amount of time spent on copying and distribution, she developed routing slips for the nursing home administrator to use in disseminating information to staff.

- To ensure that phones are covered at all times, the telephones for the Administration Department are call-forwarded to the Information Desk at the end of the day to provide coverage until 9 p.m. Additionally, the Information Desk telephones are call-forwarded to Administration from 8:00 a.m. to 8:30 a.m. since Information Desk employees don't begin their workday until 8:30 a.m.

- For years, folders were used for all board and board committee meeting packets. To save costs, she approached the CEO for his approval in eliminating the folders and using paper clips instead. The cost variance was $.25 for one hundred clips versus $11.31 for twenty-five folders (she normally ordered fifty folders each month for her meetings alone, plus in the Health System, there were approximately twenty regular meetings per month.) She shared this information with all the admins, and folders were eliminated for meetings throughout the Health System.

CAN JUGGLE TASKS

Does this sound like anyone you know?

> *Our admin began her day by looking at the incoming mail. The first letter she opened was from a vendor, who used a word she'd never heard before. She looked the word up in the dictionary and then realized the dictionary cover was a bit soiled. She got up to get soap and water from the restroom but while she was there, she noticed she'd forgotten to apply lipstick that morning. Of course, she had to return to her desk to get the lipstick and then return to the restroom to use the mirror. A colleague came in, and the two began speaking about an upcoming conference. The colleague asked the admin to fax her a copy of the program for the conference. When she returned to her desk, she went through her files and located the program, but she didn't have the fax number for her colleague. She called the receptionist to find it and was reminded that today was the day the computer class was being held. The admin tried to find her registration form for the computer class but couldn't. She decided to call the training department to see if she had in fact registered. The moment she hung up the phone, she remembered that she still hadn't sent the fax. As she got up to go to the fax machine, she noticed that her "file pile" was growing to a precarious height. She began to file the paper when she saw...*

The ability to handle several different things simultaneously is a feature of the creative personality. To illustrate, many authors can work on three different books in a given day. To be writing five or six books simultaneously, to have concurrent works-in-progress, is not unusual among those who write for a living. Such a work style, though, would cause circuits to overload in some individuals. Can you increase your tolerance for handling multiple projects simultaneously? Yes—but only if you wish to do so. The key is to find a balance by being disciplined and organized and by learning to prioritize. The following two exercises will provide you with some practice.

EXERCISE:

Assess your working style.

Answer the following questions to learn more about your working style—are you mono-focused or multi-focused? Check "yes" or "no" in response to each question:

Yes _____ No _____ 1. Do you prefer a "monochromatic" look to your attire?

Yes _____ No _____ 2. Do you rearrange the furniture in your home or office at least once every six months?

Yes _____ No _____ 3. Do you try out a new recipe from a cookbook at least once a month?

Yes _____ No _____ 4. Do you use "waiting" time to do something else? (For example, do you read while waiting in line?)

Yes _____ No _____ 5. Do you get annoyed by interruptions such as a phone call?

Yes _____ No _____ 6. Do you feel you have improved your mind in the last week?

Yes _____ No _____ 7. Do you know what kind of learner you are?

Yes _____ No _____ 8. Do you finish one project before starting another?

Yes _____ No _____ 9. Do you frequently have the radio or television on while you work?

Yes _____ No _____ 10. Do you believe you could excel in several different types of jobs?

Give yourself ten points for every "yes" answer you had except for questions #1, #5, and #8 (allow no points for your answer to these three questions—no matter what your answer was).

Your score? _____

A score of "70" means you're quite facile at handling multiple interests at virtually the same time. This is a trait of creative people and also a trait of successfully busy people. Life is seldom so accommodating that it gives us the luxury of doing only one thing at a time. We are usually bombarded with demands—the demands of time, of people, of life itself. It would be wonderful to be able to neatly pigeonhole each responsibility, finish it with a flourish, and then move on in lockstep fashion to the next responsibility. But such a schedule is an unrealistic one. Learn to adjust to interruptions, learn to juggle multiple priorities, learn to accommodate multiple bosses. The next exercise provides a tool for doing just that.

EXERCISE:

Make IT a priority.

The IT technique forces you to think of two significant aspects of your working day: Intentions and Time. Begin by making a list of all the things you intend to do today. Separate your Intentions list according to things you intend to do and the calls you intend to make.

Things to do   **Calls to make**

1. _____   _____

2. _____   _____

3. _____   _____

4. _____   _____

5. _____   _____

6. _____   _____

7. _____   _____

8. _____   _____

9. _____   _____

10. _____   _____

Now let the Time factor help you prioritize. What *must* you do today? What will you do if time permits?

Use the diagram on the following page to help you sort it all out.

Must DO Today	Must CALL Today
DO if Time Allows	CALL if Time Allows

INTERVIEW:

Roberta L. Carter, CPS, office of the Vice President of Human Resources, Production Systems Group, Xerox Corporation, Rochester, New York

Q: *Given these traits, which do you feel is most important for administrative professionals and why?*

A: **Is self-confident**—You need to know yourself. Know what things will cause you to react and how well you handle pressure.

Is resourceful—Determine who, what, and where to go for information that will assist your customer/clients if you don't have the answer. Pointing the customer/client in the right direction always results in benefits to you and the business.

Is self-directed—With time of the essence, you cannot wait to be told what to do. You need to be able to envision problems and start working toward a solution/answer. This involves taking the initiative to handle matters before they become major. It also involves handling the small tasks so your manager/supervisor can focus on strategic plans instead of routine tasks.

Can juggle tasks—Having the ability to "juggle tasks" can carry you a long way in your career. This particular skill plays a major role in the administrative position. It entails flexibility and prioritization—much-needed and highly valued traits in the work environment today—especially when changes happen on a minute-to-minute and daily basis.

Q: *How do you handle the stress associated with your job?*

A: Currently I support the Vice President of Human Resources in the Production Systems Group (PSG) at Xerox. My job entails handling correspondence to Human Resource Operations Managers and correspondence to the president of the organization and his direct reports. The contents of the correspondence include high-level compensation results, interview feedback of high-level candidates, job competencies and skills, minutes of various project teams, etc. In addition, I perform routine filing of personnel and confidential information; handle travel arrangements, purchase requisitions, and check requests for payments of miscellaneous office supplies, books, and recognition items.

In addition, I serve on several project teams—i.e. Records Management Coordinators Network, Xerox Dinner Award Team, the Emergency Preparedness Team and Zero Injury Team for the PSG Governance area (comprised of direct reports to the president and their administrative assistants).

I relieve stress in the office by ensuring that I take mini-breaks (five minutes or less) from my desk at least a couple of times in the morning and afternoon. After work, I enjoy music, reading, and even taking a shopping break prior to arriving at my destination. (This may include just browsing through the card section at the local grocery store or window-shopping at my favorite boutique). Spending Saturday morning having coffee with friends; attending social functions such as weddings and family events; and participating in religious conferences—these are other ways I relieve stress. For me, my faith in God has kept me focused. It gives me the right perspective to help me balance and prioritize all the activities in my life.

Q: *It's been said that results depend on relationships. What suggestions to you have for optimizing one's relationship with one's manager and other key players at work?*

A: I always look at what's best for the customer and what impact the results of my relationship will have on the customer/client. Long-term relationships are important to me and to my company as well. I extend this perspective to my work with peers and supervisors. In order to optimize your relationships with customers, co-workers, and/or clients and speakers, you must realize that relationships with customers determine their decision to keep on being customers. Keeping this in mind will always yield the best results and will positively impact bottom-line profit.

Q: *What macrocosmic challenges facing the world may be microcosmically affecting the way you work?*

A: Technological inventions in the future will microcosmically affect the way we work. I envision smaller computers and accessories that carry huge volumes of information, easily accessible via digital touch and high-speed connections. Information can be accessed within a "nanosecond." It will change processes in the medical/health fields, manufacturing, and human resource, to name a few. Innovations will also catapult changes in federal and state laws. Technology will revolutionize the way information is processed and disseminated, will impact ways even household chores are carried out, and will effect changes in eating habits, among other things.

Q: The only constant, it seems, is change. In some organizations, in fact, the descriptive sentence is "No sooner said ... than changed!" What can administrative professionals do to accept—perhaps even embrace—change.

A: Being a proponent of administrative/secretarial certification and having coordinated/taught programs to enable other administrative professionals to attain their certification, I have encouraged others to accept change by helping them embark on educational/certification programs. These certification journeys empower co-workers mentally and technically to embrace change.

Networking is another activity that I have urged others to establish. Extending your circle of acquaintances helps you interact with other ethnic and professional groups so that you acquire a "rest-of-the-world" view and can more easily function in other cultures.

Q: What "lessons learned" can you share with others on how to be a "frontline superstar"?

A: I'd like to share these lessons with those who want to become "frontline superstars:"

- I have learned that—despite all one's technical abilities/skills—attitude is a highly valued trait. So, too, are interpersonal skills.
- I have learned that taking initiative to "jump start" a process, procedure, or task is a good thing.
- I have learned that networking plays a large role in gaining access to avenues for acquiring a new job or making decisions for the future.
- I have learned that "humor" helps to alleviate stress in the workplace and in one's personal life.

- I have learned to be "consistent" and "persistent" when embarking on new goals or objectives, whether personal or professional.

- I have learned that continuous learning is an "asset" and not a "liability."

The above lessons will benefit you if you take advantage of educational opportunities. These opportunities include membership in professional associations, religious activities, attending social events, conferences for continuous learning, and networking.

Q: *What advice can you give regarding updating one's skills?*

A: By constantly upgrading technical skills, learning new software packages, and embracing knowledge, you can best apply your natural talents. Having a mentor with whom you can discuss future trends, etc. is also a plus. Keeping apprized of trends in your profession can prepare you for what the future holds.

Technology is impacting the administrative professional's role in that the traditional tasks of typing correspondence, handling routine mail, etc. are no longer a major function of the administrative professional's role. This role now encompasses drafting of complex correspondence, handling databases, and understanding organizational hierarchy. Being "politically savvy" is another component of the administrative professional's role that needs to be further understood.

I believe frontline professionals of the future will have to be highly skilled in order to handle more complex job assignments. They will be involved with project management, will be asked to participate in various taskforces, will be continuous customer-liaisons, and will have the responsibility of getting prolific amounts of information disseminated in a timely manner. Those who have these skills will not only be regarded as superstars—they will be much sought after.

THINKS FLUIDITY

"Verbal fluidity" refers to the ability to find the words you need *when you need them*. The more quickly ideas pop into your head, the more readily you can make decisions and solve problems (*and* sound articulate in job interviews!). With practice, you can develop the skill of generating ideas quickly. But if you are tense, it will be much harder to get into the playful frame of mind required for brainstorming and bouncing ideas around.

EXERCISE:

Practice verbal skills.

There are more than a million words in the English language. Alas, most people depend on the same old few over and over. Further, we don't use those familiar few in novel ways. This exercise is designed to help you to savor the flavor of new verbal entrees.

Can you think of a refreshingly new, non-trite way to express the following?

1. An advertisement for a photographer who takes pictures of children and animals:

    _____

    _____

    _____

2. A description of Margaret Thatcher's strength-coupled-with-femininity:

    _____

    _____

    _____

3. An announcement to keep drinking under control during the holidays:

    _____

    _____

    _____

4. An advertisement for a tennis equipment store:

_____

_____

5. An advertisement for a radio talk show of substance, not idle talk:

_____

_____

6. An advertisement for a skilled plumber:

_____

_____

7. A word to suggest that Bill and Hillary Clinton function as a single entity:

_____

_____

8. A judge's exhortation to students participating in a Math Olympics contest:

_____

_____

9. An advertisement for a bank hoping to attract new female customers:

_____

_____

Possible answers. 1. Prints Charming 2. An iron fist inside a velvet glove 3. "Eat, think, and be merry." 4. The Merchant of Tennis 5. Mind over chatter 6. "At your disposal" 7. Billary 8. "May the best math win!" 9. "Girls just wanna have funds."

EXERCISE:

Stratify.

Stratification is a tool from the world of Total Quality Management (TQM). Teams (and individuals too) use this tool to help discern emerging patterns or trends among seemingly unrelated pieces of information. It can help you to move easily and fluidly among data that may seem disparate at first glance.

Assume that your team has conducted a survey among employees and found that survey participants identified the following as the most common causes of poor morale:

- No one listens

- Meetings don't start on time

- No socializing beyond work

- Projects always take longer than we're led to believe

- Restrooms are never clean

- Teams aren't given the support they need

- Never see the bosses

- Too much pressure, too much stress

- Employees expect managers to have all the answers

- Poor communication

- Managers don't care

- Offices are sterile

- Employees don't care

- Teams aren't given enough direction

- No suggestion program

- We never know what's going on

- Limited cafeteria menu

If you were to stratify or categorize these items, one stratification could easily be Communications. Under it would be listed "No one listens," "Poor communication," "Teams aren't given enough direction," and "We never know what's going on."

What other stratifications would you make and which items would you place in each? (Note: On occasion, an item might fit in more than one stratification.)

HAS ORIGINAL THOUGHTS

O ne very tough question job interviewers sometimes use is this: "What was your last original thought?"

How would you answer that one? What is the last totally original idea you had?

Most applicants are thrown off guard by this question. Even after they regain their composure, however, they are still unable to provide an answer. Sensitize yourself to this question and several times a day, ask yourself, "Have I had any totally original thoughts lately?"

Keep a notebook reserved just for recording your original thoughts. Two exercises that encourage original thought are provided on the following pages.

EXERCISE:

Encourage wild thinking.

Where does wild thinking come from? It's usually sparked by an association that may be quite remote. For example, do you think managers could learn something by studying caterpillars? Read the following, and then see whether you'd answer the same way the second time:

> French botanist Henri Fabre discovered something very unusual about "processionary" caterpillars. If he put one down on the ground and lined up a dozen others behind the first, the caterpillars would begin going in a circle—round and round, all of them quite contentedly following the one ahead of them. He wondered what would happen if he put food in the center of the procession. Would any of the caterpillars break out of the circle to get at the food? To his surprise, the caterpillars continued to follow the leader—to their death! Even though salvation was only inches away, not a single one "broke rank" to get at the nourishment.

As you read the Fabre story, you could no doubt draw parallels to the business world. Focus on the secretarial position—of today, of yesterday, of tomorrow—and, as you do, read over the following historical facts. Allow one of them to merge with your thoughts about your profession. The result should be an original thought.

> In 1484, the Portuguese navigator Diego Cam discovered the mouth of the Congo River.

> In 1499, Perkin Warbeck tried to escape from the Tower of London.

> In 1504, Henry VII placed English guilds/tradesmen under the supervision of the Crown.

In 1507, Orlando Galla of Venice improved the manufacture of glass mirrors.

In 1518, spectacles were created for shortsighted people.

In 1523, the first marine insurance policies were issued in Florence.

In 1539, the first public lottery was held in France.

In 1556, Lutherans were granted equal rights with Catholics via the Peace of Augsburg.

In 1596, Galileo invented the thermometer.

In 1606, an extensive program of road building was begun in France.

In 1612, the last recorded burning of heretics in England occurred.

In 1613, copper coins came into use.

In 1619, William Harvey discovered the circulation of blood.

Some "wild thinking" that might evolve from these historical facts:

1484:   Perhaps admins need to go on a retreat, as managers do (or at the least, get off-site training), to make plans for the future.

1499:   How many admins leave (escape) the company each year? A study could be done to compare the cost of raises to the cost of replacements.

1504:   Do admins need their own union?

1507:   What are our mirror images (admins in other organizations) doing to improve their lot? Benchmarking could be established.

1518:   Are we being shortsighted about our profession? Have we ever spoken to a futurist to learn where our profession is heading?

Explain fully your original thought about administrative professionals (past, present, or future) based on one of the other historical prompts:

_____

_____

_____

_____

_____

_____

_____

_____

_____

_____

_____

_____

_____

_____

_____

EXERCISE:

Use models.

A variety of innovation models are helping employees become original thinkers, to improve upon the old and even invent the new. (If you're interested, you can even create models of your own—simply analyze your last several innovations or imaginative contributions and define how you came up with the good idea.) The M3 Model (Moan, Magic, Merge) is a helpful, user-friendly tool. It works like this:

(M1) Moan: What in the current environment is something people are "moaning" about? What is a frequent complaint? A source of annoyance? Some bothersome reality?

(For example, in the pre-computer era, admins who needed multiple copies of a document used carbon paper, which was messy and yielded fuzzy copies. Worst of all, though, was the difficulty of correcting mistakes. An eraser or strips of correction tape were used to cover up—not very successfully—the typographical error.)

What is an organizational moan where you work? _____

_____

_____

(M2) Magic: What magic would be needed to solve the organizational moan you identified above? _____

_____

_____

(In the case of your predecessors, one clever woman thought, "If only I had a little bit of white paint, I could cover up these errors and no one would ever know they were there.")

(M3) Merge: What elements of the magical solution could actually be applied to the workplace? How could you condense, combine, expand, or modify the magical solution to fit your set of circumstances? (The can of white paint, in the previous example, was condensed to a small bottle. And—just as there are different colors of paint, it was not long before there were different colors of "white out.")

Your refined solution: _____

_____

_____

_____

_____

_____

_____

USES
METAPHORS

Jose Ortega y Gasset regarded the metaphor as "probably the most fertile power possessed by man." What is this fertile power of the imagination that allows us to bring force and color and imagery to our communications? It is simply a comparison between two things not usually compared.

The metaphor is a tool you can use to capture a far-reaching concept and express it in concrete, easily understood terms. In a study of leaders, Warren Bennis and Burt Nanus found, "A lot of our leaders had a penchant for metaphor, if not for models."

Use a metaphor to translate the complexity of an idea into the simplicity of something practical. Expressing your ideas in metaphoric terms often helps your listeners to grasp a concept more readily. Metaphors are user-friendly, which is why so many leaders employ them. Think of Winston Churchill's reference to the "Iron Curtain," or Jesse Jackson's reference to the "Rainbow Coalition," or Ann Morrison's reference to the "Glass Ceiling." Just as Einstein used the image of a slab of marble to explain a concept in Euclidean geometry, you too can use the net of a metaphor to capture an imagining and bring it into view.

EXERCISE:

Engage in metaphoric thinking.

A metaphor, as you might remember from your high school English class, is simply a comparison between two things not usually compared.

Look at the following animals and accompanying facts. Select one (or one of your own, if you like) and use it as a metaphor to describe an organizational problem. Then, extend the metaphor to find a solution.

Animal Facts

1. **Elephant:** Lives in large family units although the adult male is a solitary creature. Communicates with a "rumbling" in its throat as well as with a loud trumpeting sound. Has soft, padded feet, enabling it to move about almost noiselessly despite its size. Seldom attacks enemies. Travels widely in herds but remains close to water.

2. **Giraffe:** Has a unique pattern on its hide— no two "spots" are alike. Flexible front legs allow it to lower its head in order to drink. Elastic blood vessels regulate flow of blood to head, thus preventing loss of consciousness. Can easily camouflage itself. Has very strong skull, which protects it during head-butting. Males neck-wrestle for dominance but seldom hurt each other.

Secrets of the Frontline Superstars

3. **Jaguar:** Remains alone except for breeding season. Is considered an endangered species. Can survive in many different habitats. Does not roar. Known to attack and kill humans, but also just to follow them until they leave its territory.

4. **Ape:** Displays a wide range of emotions with body language. Is social and nurturing. Sleeps in trees at night for protection. Little competition for females. Is skilled at problem solving, recognizes itself in a mirror, suffers human maladies.

The problem-free organization does not exist. Many companies regard problems, in fact, as opportunities for improvement. Specify an organizational problem (opportunity) here—but describe it in metaphoric terms. For example, if you select an alligator, you might say, "Our problem could be compared to an alligator—its danger is masked by its sluggishness. Similarly, our individual and collective inertia is masking a danger. If we do not change, if we do not embrace the new technology, we will soon be trapped—and devoured—in the jaws of obsolescence."

One problem in my organization, depicted metaphorically: _____

_____

_____

A possible solution, depicted metaphorically: _____

_____

_____

EXERCISE:

Use the metaphor as a springboard.

Jonas Salk, in describing what led him to the polio vaccine, admitted that he learned to think as Mother Nature would think. He asked himself, "How would Nature solve this problem?"

Build your imaginative powers with this exercise. Begin by defining some aspect of your job or the profession as a whole that you feel warrants improvement—the respect that secretaries are accorded, for example, or the pay they earn.

A. What area do you feel needs improvement? _____

_____

_____

_____

_____

B. Now, as you read through the metaphor categories below, list the first five words that come into your mind:

Category	Related Words
• Nature	1. _____
	2. _____
	3. _____
	4. _____
	5. _____

• Sports

1. _____

2. _____

3. _____

4. _____

5. _____

• Cooking

1. _____

2. _____

3. _____

4. _____

5. _____

• Entertainment

1. _____

2. _____

3. _____

4. _____

5. _____

C. Now select one of the categories in Part B and think within it. Try to solve the problem you described in Part A in terms of one of the words you've listed for the category. If the solution is not coming to you, select another person or thing or even another category. Continue doing this (perhaps even making up categories of your own) until you come across an idea you think will work.

Use this formula: "If I think as (<u>insert word from a category</u>) would think, one possible solution to the problem of (<u>insert problem from Part A</u>) would be (<u>your solution</u>)."

Now you try it:

If I think as _____ would think, one possible solution

to the problem of _____

_____

would be _____

_____

_____

_____

_____

_____

_____

PROBES
IDEAS DEEPLY

N obel Prize-winning biochemist Albert Szent-Gyorgyi asserted that "discovery consists of looking at the same thing as everyone else and thinking something different."

The former secretary to Supreme Court Justice Ruth Bader Ginsburg looked at the same thing her boss looked at and yet saw something else. Justice Bader acknowledges her debt to her admin for her switch from the term "sex discrimination" to the more equitable "gender discrimination": "I owe it all to my secretary at Columbia Law School, who said, 'I'm typing all these briefs and articles for you and the word "sex," "sex," "sex" is on every page. Don't you know that those nine men (on the Supreme Court)—they hear that word, and their first association is not the way you want them to be thinking? Why don't you use the word "gender"? It is a grammatical term, and it will ward off distracting associations.' "

Innovation is preceded by a willingness to change and make changes. It is also preceded by the ability to "look at the same thing as everyone else," and yet to think something different. This power of the imagination, in the words of Bernadine Waters and Teiana McPike, support staff personnel from Johnson Controls, Inc., makes us "capable of reaching beyond existing reality."

If Jonas Salk viewed himself as both a scientist and naturalist, ask yourself what else you are—in addition to being an administrative professional. This extension beyond the literal will help you broaden the scope of your thinking.

EXERCISE:

Accept input from anywhere.

Are you blocking your own creative potential? Answer the following questions to find out. Be as honest as possible—the survey won't provide any insight unless you approach it with an open attitude. If you cover up the truth, you can't uncover the barriers blocking your imaginative capacity.

Answer each question on the basis of   1 = Never;   2 = Seldom;
3 = Often;   4 = Always.

1. ____ I am stimulated by complex problems.

2. ____ I experiment with unusual combinations.

3. ____ My colleagues think of me as a source of innovative ideas.

4. ____ I read voraciously, both in and outside my field.

5. ____ I associate with people who have decidedly different viewpoints or orientations.

6. ____ I search for better ways of doing things.

7. ____ I am asked for my opinion on tough-to-solve situations.

8. ____ I entertain new ideas with enthusiasm rather than cynicism.

9. ____ I scold myself for thinking absurd thoughts.

10. ____ I make decisions after considering a number of possibilities.

11. ____ I ask a lot of questions.

12. ____ I worry about appearing foolish.

13. ____ I enjoy learning new things.

14. ____ I encourage open discussion.

15. ____ I believe disagreeing can be healthy.

16. ____ I like to have my thinking challenged.

17. ____ I believe logic can solve every problem.

18. ____ I am impatient with rigid problem-solvers.

19. ____ I am mentally playful.

20. ____ I follow rules and recipes to the letter.

21. ____ I daydream.

22. ____ I like/understand expressions such as "Architecture is frozen music."

23. ____ I can see why Peter Drucker advised a would-be executive to learn to play the violin.

24. ____ I engage in what Einstein termed "wildly speculative thinking."

25. ____ I synthesize pieces of knowledge into new entities.

A "perfect" score for the perfect innovator would be 88—four points for every question except #9, #12, #17, and #20 (each of which would earn only one point). However, as there are no perfect people, think of your score as being on a continuum. No matter where you placed, pledge to acquire more of the innovator's traits by engaging in some of the behaviors suggested here—allowing yourself more daydreaming time, for example.

EXERCISE:

Make work fun.

A number of management gurus—Tom Peters, W. Edwards Deming, Michael LeBoeuf—assert that work should be fun, that if we enjoy what we do, we'll do it better. Perhaps in support of this tenet or perhaps because the opposite of fun (excessive stress) can diminish productivity, a number of organizations are forming "joy gangs." A joy gang is a team that meets regularly to discover ways to make the workplace a more enjoyable place to be. On the surface, it may seem that work is not supposed to be fun, but the truth is we are willing to work harder when we take pleasure in our work place and our work mates.

Assume that the leader of your joy gang has asked you and the other members of the team to prepare a list of fifteen ways to bring joy to the workplace. What would you put on your list?

1. _____
2. _____
3. _____
4. _____
5. _____
6. _____
7. _____
8. _____
9. _____
10. _____

11. _____

12. _____

13. _____

14. _____

15. _____

Which of the ideas on your list are you most likely to attempt to implement? _____

_____

_____

_____

_____

What might keep you from implementing them? _____

_____

_____

_____

_____

_____

BRAVELY NON-CONFORMS

There is an undeniable security in knowing that we don't stand alone. And yet, avant-garde thinkers and innovators have always had to stand on their own, at least at some point. The average follower will not leave the fold, or the old, until the fold itself is embracing the new. Before that happens, however, the leader remains a lone voice, a visionary who must suffer the "slings and arrows" of nonacceptance.

It takes courage to step outside existing boundaries. It requires self-confidence to stand by your plan and await the endorsement of others.

EXERCISE:

Use your multiple facets.

Innovative administrative professionals know they are much more, and can be much more, than the label of their job titles. There is more they can do if they choose not to conform to their standard responsibilities. Even if you don't have the power to change your official designation, you might create an unofficial designation. Consider what one admin in Flagstaff, Arizona, did: she proclaimed herself "Czarina of the Coffee Room." Since she was responsible for collecting money for and purchasing coffee supplies, she decided to turn her supplemental responsibility into a sphere of influence. She began signing her memos (regarding the coffee collections) and notices in the coffee room with her new title. In her own creative way, she brought levity into the lives of many people and reduced somewhat the onerous aspects of being in charge of coffee.

Here is a list of "personas" that members of effective support staff teams use to describe themselves. The list was compiled by support staff personnel from Johnson Controls, Inc.: Sandy Hagemann, Jenn Lisser, Patty Kachelski, Dawn Tietyen, Sue Wisnewski, Carol Ryan, Barbara Nenorth, Carol Matter, Bonnie Lenz, Eileen Burkman, and Cathy McCash.

Leader	Idealist
Devil's advocate	Facilitator
Minister	Timekeeper
Surgeon	Delegator
Analyzer	Peacekeeper
Instigator	Nominator
Scribe	Genius

Problem solver	Dreamer
Cheerleader	Presenter
Babysitter	Designer
Confidence builder	Marketer
Seller	Authority figure

You are, we all are, many different people rolled into one unique entity. Unfortunately, many of us ignore the possibilities lying within us; we fail to break down boundaries and probe the personas we are and can be.

What additional roles do you play as you perform your job?

_____

_____

_____

_____

_____

Which personas are you best at? _____

_____

_____

Which do you most need to improve? _____

_____

_____

EXERCISE:

Be "disobedient."

Admins are often advised to dress for the next-level position they wish to hold. If there's merit in that advice, there's also merit in the advice to learn managerial skills in order to take on more managerial tasks. But whom do *managers* take advice from? Very often, it's people like guru Tom Peters who influence managers most. One of the things Mr. Peters tells managers is this: "If you have gone a whole week without being disobedient, you are doing yourself and your organization a disservice."

Of course, by "disobedient," he doesn't mean breaking the rules just to break the rules. Rather, consider what practices are currently being engaged in. Analyze the work processes currently being followed and then suggest ways to improve upon those practices and processes—to change them for the better.

If you really want to be a superstar, if you really want to make change happen, you must acknowledge that power does not flow to invisible people. To improve upon existing practices and processes, you may need more power than you currently have. To get it, you must be pro-active: you cannot cling to the wall like a flower. You must come to the forefront to see and be seen. Here are tips for self- and plan-promotion. You probably will not be comfortable with all of them. Place a checkmark in front of those you may need help doing.

___ Volunteer for projects that no one else want or no one else is doing— especially those projects that will get you noticed by those who can help advance your idea.

___ Write an article about your idea. Yes, you can submit it to the agency newsletter but why not think big and submit it, for example, to a business magazine?

___ Accept credit (or ask for it) and praise without embarrassment.

___ Make a presentation about your improvement-plan at a staff meeting. Or, if it's a "big, hairy, audacious goal," make the presentation at the next conference your department is holding.

___ Plan on spending five minutes every Monday morning (other mornings, too, if possible), keeping your manager apprised of your plans for the week.

___ Become identified with a phrase you coined (the Czarina of Customer Service) or a thing you do or an article of clothing you wear. Remember President Reagan's jellybeans? Sally Jesse Raphael's red glasses? Ideally, your hallmark will be related to the passion you feel for your particular improvement-project.

___ Develop an expertise so that when decision-makers and clout-carriers need it, they know where to turn.

___ Show appreciation, if only in the form of a greeting card, to all those who go out of their way to assist you. Form alliances.

INTERVIEW:

Eleanor Bautista, Charlotte Easter, Jennifer Martinez, Angela Robinson and Yvonne Young-Dong, Human Resource Service Center, Southwest, Department of the Navy, San Diego, California

Q: *Given these traits, which do you feel is most important for administrative professionals and why?*

A: Some of the important traits an administrative professional should have are self-confidence, ability to defer judgment, and receptivity to new ideas. When one portrays a certain level of self-confidence, supervisors and colleagues are more willing to accept and listen to that person's ideas. One should also be receptive to new ideas since change is inevitable and new ideas can inspire. If a person is receptive to new ideas, he or she is more likely to be called upon when special needs arise in their organization. Supervisors typically remember those who have worked on projects and helped generate novel ideas that helped the organization.

Finally, a person should have the ability to treat others in a professional manner, whether they are supervisors or co-workers. Front-line personnel cannot judge a metaphoric book by its cover. When a person pre-judges others based on appearance or the way they speak, others will respond to the way they are perceived and will act accordingly.

Having all of these traits helps one stand out as a front-line employee in their organization.

Q: *How do you handle the stress associated with your job?*

A: There are many different ways one can handle stress on the job. The best way to avoid stress is to call in sick! On a serious note, remind yourself that your health is very important, and if your job is becoming too stressful, the stress will affect your health. You can do a number of things to help alleviate tension. First, take a short break, take a walk around the block, or get a breath of fresh air. Then come back and refocus.

Additionally, you can talk to someone, either your supervisor or co-workers. Sometimes talking about what is stressful lightens the mood, even if it can't lighten the workload. Another stress release can be humor: don't take things too seriously. Bring laughter in and share it.

Get organized, prioritize your work, make a list and stick to it. The feeling that you are in control of your job will alleviate some of the stress associated with it. As you begin to cross completed items off your list, you'll experience a real sense of accomplishment.

To summarize, organize, prioritize, and break the work down into small pieces.

Q: *It's been said that results depend on relationships. What suggestions to you have for optimizing one's relationship with one's manager and other key players at work?*

A: The best ways to optimize one's relationship with managers and other key players in the work place is to genuinely care about the people on your team and respect the opinions of others. Establish a good working relationship with your co-workers and with management by having open communication, by addressing problems when they occur, and by meeting with management to ensure everyone is working towards the same goal.

Always actively listen without formulating questions in your mind while someone else is speaking. Otherwise, you may miss details or important information. Offer assistance when needed and manage your time wisely.

Finally, demonstrate loyalty and respect for one another. Actively use the golden rule: Treat others as you would like to be treated. This is key to positive results.

Q: *What macrocosmic challenges facing the nation may be microcosmically affecting the way today's administrative professionals work?*

A: Terrorism is an ever-present danger in our nation today. When terrorism occurs, war follows. With war comes the fact that troops will be called or recalled to duty. Further, when companies downsize, they create a smaller workforce without reducing the amount of work.

With these macrocosmic challenges facing our nation, the microcosmic effects on today's administrative professional are numerous and powerful.

Security has increased throughout the nation—on the physical and the technical levels as well. With this increased attention to possible attacks, employees have the increased responsibility to report security breaches and/or suspicious activity.

Q: *The only constant, it seems, is change. In some organizations, in fact, the descriptive sentence is "No sooner said ... than changed!" What can administrative professionals do to accept—perhaps even embrace—change?*

A: Administrative professionals need to accept the fact that change is going to happen. Regardless of situations in family life, work, church or yourself, change is going to come. Do not slip into denial. Once you realize and accept the idea of change, be flexible. If

Secrets of the Frontline Superstars

you are not, change can negatively impact your mental, emotional and physical health. Be prepared to perform at your best wherever you are needed. If you do not know how to do something, ask for help, express appreciation and remember what you've learned.

With technology changing at a tremendous speed, administrative professionals need to remain marketable in this ever-changing company of life. To do so, they must update skills as often as possible by volunteering for special jobs and by requesting training. Realize and accept the fact that the system or processes you are working on today will most likely be rewritten or obsolete in five years or fewer.

Put forth the effort to research the skills needed to make success occur. Volunteer, lead, be assertive, and show concern for the mission, regardless of your position, your input is valuable to that mission. Embrace change; it is a part of life.

 What "lessons learned" can you share with others on how to be a "frontline superstar"?

A frontline superstar is self-confident, flexible, organized, and always ready to work on special projects within the organization. Such individuals also bring new ideas to the table and help find ways to do things more efficiently. When going to supervisors with your ideas, you must project self-confidence

Frontline superstars are organized, allowing them to answer questions and assist others. Also, they think on their feet and respond in a moment's notice. Finally, a frontline superstar is always flexible. She may be overworked but always give the impression that she has time to assist customers and co-workers.

Q: What advice can you give regarding updating one's skills?

A: Life is a journey in which we are constantly learning—whether we realize it or not. Along that journey we work and learn new skills. To keep our minds sharp and our job interesting, we need to update our skills regularly. If you keep your skills up-to-date, new opportunities will invariably open up for you.

CONCLUSION

We are living in times of tremendous turmoil, tremendous change. And the pace of change will continue at astonishing levels. When you consider that many administrative professionals transitioned from typewriters to computer keyboards, you have a sense of the powerful impact of technology on office life. Such impacts will continue—at ever-greater speeds and with ever-greater impacts.

It's imagination that drives those changes—and in this information era, the most valuable employees will be those who continuously acquire relevant information and apply it to produce innovative outcomes.

The information contained in the preceding pages was presented to share with you traits of imaginative individuals, believing that creativity, like most other traits, can be developed. The exercises associated with each trait offer practice in refining your existing skills and exploring those you haven't yet acquired. Sharpening those creative skills will lead to the vision needed for innovation. That vision, however, needs nurturing—nurturing to develop the art of imagining. As Jonathan Swift declared, "Vision is the art of seeing things invisible."

Can you answer "yes" to at least one of these questions?

- Do you view chaos as a possible source of dynamic thought?

- Do you seek information from multiple sources?

- Are you willing to try new things?

- Have you experienced the "magic of thinking big"?

If you can, then you have learned your lessons well. Know that others, wondrously successful others, are also answering "yes" to the same questions. (Witness the "BHAGs" established by Wal-Mart founder, Sam Walton. These "Big Hairy Audacious Goals" drove him to make his first store the most profitable one in the whole state within a five-year period). You should be ready now to set some BHAGs of your own.

Those BHAGs will lead to having greater visibility focused on your competencies. Accept the challenges and be guided by your confidence—in yourself, in your ideas, in your team, and in your ability to make a difference.

Admins hold a pivotal place in the organizational hierarchy. As they assume responsibilities more managerial in nature, so will they assume higher levels of empowerment and recompense. Because the traditional "command-and-control" style of management is being discarded in many places, solutions to problems are welcomed from all levels of the organization. With a growing increase of "open-book" management thinking, admins are privy to more knowledge than ever before. And knowledge, of course, is power.

The time is ripe for the innovative administrative professionals to seize that power and seize the moment too. With innovative thinking, an admin can alter the course of his or her own destiny and the course of the profession as well.

BIBLIOGRAPHY AND SUGGESTED READING

American Heritage Dictionaries, Editor. *The New Office Professional's Handbook: How to Survive and Thrive in Today's Office Environment.* Houghton Mifflin Co. , August 2001.

Aslett, Don. *The Office Clutter Cure: How to Get Out from Under It All!* Betterway Publications, March 1995.

Beckel, Heather. *Be a Kickass Assistant.* Warner Books. 1st edition, May 2002.

Bly, Robert. *The Encyclopedia of Business Letters, Fax Memos, and E-Mail.* Career Press, 1st edition, April 1999.

Burke, Michelle Marie. *The Valuable Office Professional: For Administrative Assistants, Office Managers, Secretaries, and Other Support Staff.* AMACOM Books, October 1996.

DeVries, Mary. *The Professional Secretary's Handbook.* Houghton Mifflin Co., 3rd edition, October 1995.

Duncan, Melba. *The New Executive Assistant: Advice for Succeeding in Your Career.* McGraw-Hill, February 1997.

Eisenberg, Ronni. *Organize Your Office!: Simple Routines for Managing Your Workspace.* Hyperion Books, January 1999.

Eisenberg, Ronni. *The Overwhelmed Person's Guide to Time Management.* Plume Press, January 1997.

Hooper, Cindy. *The Official Secretary's Guide to Sanity and Survival.* July Publishing, April 2001.

Jasper, Jan. *Take Back Your Time: How to Regain Control of Work, Information, and Technology.* Griffin Trade Paperback, October 1999.

Jean, Anna-Carin. *The Organizer: Secrets & Systems from the World's Top Executive Assistants.* McGraw-Hill Trade, February 1997.

Lizotte, Ken. *From Secretary Track to Fast Track: The Great Ahead Guide for Administrative Assistants, Secretaries, Office Managers, Receptionists,* and *Everyone who Wants More.* AMACOM Books, May 1996.

Quible, Zane. *Administrative Office Management.* Prentice Hall, 7th edition, June 2000.

Spencer, John. *The Professional Secretary's Handbook: Communication Skills.* Barron's Educational Series, February 1997.

Stroman, James. *Administrative Assistant's & Secretary's Handbook.* AMACOM Books, June 1995.

Tarbell, Shirley. *Administrative Assistant/Secretary Career Starter.* LearningExpress, 1st edition, January 1998.

Winston, Stephanie. *Stephanie Winston's Best Organizing Tips: Quick, Simple Ways to Get Organized and Get on With Your Life.* Fireside Press, January 1996.

Wisinski, Jerry. *Building a Partnership with Your Boss.* AMACOM Books, February 1999.

AVAILABLE FROM SKILLPATH PUBLICATIONS

12 Secrets to High Self-Esteem by Linda Larsen

Business Communication Style Guide by Michelle Fairfield Poley and Dusty Crocker

Communicating for Results by Michelle Fairfield Poley

Dealing With Different, Diverse (and Difficult) People by Barbara Braunstein

Discovering Your Purpose by Ivy Haley

Organized for Success! by Nanci McGraw

Productivity Power by Jim Temme

Stress Control by Steve Bell

Success Advantage by SkillPath Trainers

Windows Wit & Wisdom by Don R. Crawley

Notes

Notes

Notes

Secrets of the Frontline Superstars